PATH TO THE LIGHT

Kabbalah Centre Publishing is a registered DBA of Kabbalah Centre International, Inc.

For further information:

The Kabbalah Centre
155 E. 48th St., New York, NY 10017
1062 S. Robertson Blvd., Los Angeles, CA 90035

1.800.Kabbalah www.kabbalah.com

Printed in USA, January 2018

ISBN: 978-1-57189-966-8

eBook ISBN: 978-1-57189-971-2

Design: HL Design (Hyun Min Lee) www.hldesignco.com

PATH TO THE LIGHT

DECODING THE BIBLE WITH KABBALAH

KABBALAH CENTRE PUBLISHING

An Anthology of Commentary from Kabbalist **Rav Berg**

BOOK OF BERESHEET Volume 2

Vayera Chayei Sarah Toldot

PREFACE

In this volume of commentaries given on the Book of Beresheet, Rav Berg deals with the Torah portions of Vayera, Chayei Sarah, and Toldot, which respectively take the biblical narrative from the angel's announcement of Isaac's birth to Abraham and Sarah, through momentous events such as the story of Lot and the cities of Sodom and Gomorrah, the Binding of Isaac, the death and burial of Sarah, the hostility between Jacob and Esau, and culminating with Jacob's departure to dwell with his uncle, Laban.

These are some of the most significant and well-known tales recounted in the Bible. Yet, as Rav Berg continually reminds us, there is nothing whatsoever to be gained from a literal reading of such stories—except perhaps a mild entertainment and, occasionally, some potent, resounding poetry. It is a testament to the Rav's wisdom that he can take these simple, yet perplexing tales and unravel their real meaning and purpose into eternally relevant spiritual teachings and, more importantly, a spiritual technology to bring about transformation and, ultimately, closeness to the Creator. In the opening section, we learn how a simple statement of Sarah's age is deconstructed to reveal one of Kabbalah's deepest mysteries, and the vast significance of the 400 shekels paid for her gravesite in Hebron.

With characteristic sagacity and frequent good humor, the Rav shows, in the following pages, how it is possible to decode the Bible's grand saga of Patriarchs and Promised Land to uncover a timeless message embodying information about the true structure and purpose of the universe, along with instructions and methodology for leading a spiritually fruitful and rewarding life. As the Rav tells us, this information, encoded 3,400 years ago, is just as relevant today—as the nature of humanity and the world itself has not changed. Chaos is still chaos. With frequent references to, and quotations from the Zohar, as well as the Talmud, Rav Isaac Luria (the Ari), Rav Ashlag, and Rav Brandwein, the Rav reveals what kabbalists have known for thousands of years. Concepts that are only just now being discovered by contemporary quantum physics; concepts that, while being rigorously scientific, also elucidate metaphysical doctrines regarding the essentially illusionary nature of what we term reality. In some cases, such teachings entail a knowledge that is itself at the very limits of human comprehension. Yet the Rav is able to devise disarmingly straightforward and everyday ways of explicating them in understandable terms. What was once perhaps an engaging if irrelevant yarn from the very distant past becomes vital information about the purpose and meaning of our lives here and now.

Sometimes Rav Berg relates a joke; sometimes he points to the structure of a lightbulb or a car; sometimes he references the theorems of contemporary physics (which themselves increasingly resemble ideas derived from ancient kabbalistic texts); sometimes it is an anecdote from his own or Karen's life; and often he will refer to the chaotic events happening at the time of his teaching, from the growing hatred between ethnic or religious factions, to the disastrous consequences of a technology we have misused. No matter how profoundly complex his subject is, the Rav will find a way to present it in a manner so clear that a child will be able to grasp it.

Vayera is regarded as one of the most important and difficult of all Torah portions and, as readers will soon see, right off the top, the Rav plunges into his commentary by demonstrating how a few lines about Abraham contain a wisdom concerning the stages in cosmic Creation, as well as reveal the secret of the Three Column System—the only means by which negativity can be transmuted into positivity, thus solving the only problem this world and we ourselves really face.

One of the most striking things about this commentary is its relentless practicality. Although we are often dealing with the deepest metaphysical, spiritual, and scientific concerns, the Rav never fails to remind us that Kabbalah is quintessentially a technology designed to improve our lives, and with them to improve a world whose completion and perfection is in our own hands. Kabbalah, he affirms many times, is most assuredly not a religion. It is a methodology for operating our lives purposefully, and for maximizing our potential in a world of illusion, insanity, and chaos. It is said that when the student is ready the teacher appears. The world has never been more ready—and the teacher is right here in this and the other volumes, just as Kabbalah is finally here and freely available to all.

The Rav's greatness in bringing to the world a teaching designed specifically for humanity, yet for so long denied it, will one day be viewed as an axial event in human history—one that changed everything.

TABLE OF CONTENTS

BOOK OF BERESHEET:

Portion of Vayera

PORTION OF VAYERA

Beresheet 18:1 The Lord appeared to Abraham in the plains of Mamre, and he sat in the tent door in the heat of the day.

Restoring Humanity's Control Over the Universe

The Zohar says:

> Rav Chiya opened the discussion, IT IS WRITTEN, "The flowers appeared on the earth, the time of the singing of the birds has come, and the voice of the turtledove is heard in our land." (Shir Hashirim 2:12) "The flowers appeared on the earth" MEANS THAT when the Holy One, blessed be He, created the world, He endowed the earth with appropriate powers, so that everything was in the earth BUT it did not produce any fruit until Adam was created. As soon as Adam was created, everything in the earth became visible, that is, the earth began to reveal the powers and products that were implanted within it. Similarly, the Heavens did not give any powers to the Earth until humankind appeared, as it is written, "And no plant of the field was yet in the earth, and no herb of the field had yet grown, for the Lord, our God, had not caused it to rain upon the earth, and there was not a man to till the ground." (Beresheet 2:5) All the offspring and products were concealed in the earth. They did not appear, and the Heavens were prevented from pouring rain on the earth because humankind did not yet exist. Because it had not yet been created, the revelation of all things was delayed. As soon as humankind appeared, however, "The flowers appeared on the earth," and all the

hidden and concealed powers were now revealed...After Adam sinned, everything disappeared from the world, and the earth was cursed, as it is written, "Cursed is the earth for your sake." (Beresheet 3:17) "When you till the ground, it shall not henceforth give its strength to you..." When Noah appeared in the world, he prepared spades and hoes. Afterwards, however, "he drank of the wine, and was drunk; and he was uncovered within his tent." (Beresheet 9:21) And later, the people of the world sinned before the Holy One, blessed be He. And the powers of the earth disappeared again. THUS, ALL THE IMPROVEMENTS OF NOAH WERE LOST. And so it remained until Abraham appeared. As soon as Abraham appeared, "the flowers appeared on the earth." THIS MEANS THAT the powers of the earth were amended and revealed. "The time of the singing of the birds (also: 'pruning') has come," REFERRING TO THE TIME when the Holy One, blessed be He, told him to circumcise himself. THE TERM "PRUNING'" ALLUDES TO THE REMOVAL OF THE FORESKIN. Thus, the time was ripe for the covenant to appear in Abraham, MEANING when he was circumcised. Only then was the verse, "THE FLOWERS APPEARED..." fulfilled through him, and the word of the Holy One, blessed be He was revealed openly to him. As it is written, "And the Lord appeared to him," after he was circumcised.
—Zohar, Lech Lecha 1:1-6

This section of the Zohar is referring to Beresheet Two where we deal with the physical corporeal manifestation of Beresheet One. Beresheet One is thought energy-intelligence and deals with the ninety-nine percent of everything, which is obviously not physical. We want to connect to the 99 Percent Reality because this is where all the information in the cosmos actually exists.

At the time of Creation, everything was in a state of suspended animation, existing only in a potential form until Adam was created. Because of Adam everything began to sprout, to appear in movement. Adam, and only Adam, created the condition in which everything could become revealed and manifested. The Zohar states that humans control the cosmos—every animate and inanimate object in this universe. This leads us to the conclusion that we should be able to bend spoons and teleport objects. We should be able to stop the sun, as Joshua did. Moses even stopped the Red Sea from flowing. According to the Bible, these things have all happened. We may believe that they are fables and myths or we can understand that what the stories of Joshua or Moses are meant to show us is that humanity has this capacity, this potential. For most of us, however, we may try to achieve things with our minds, yet we do not succeed. We can create a thorough business plan but it can fail. This is on a physical level.

In the section quoted above, the Zohar tells us that Adam controlled the universe, and because we all come from Adam, we, too, have that same power to control all things. We can control the sun, even without any physical means to bring us into contact with the sun. With physical things, we can touch them, so to that extent we can control them. If we were meant to control everything in the universe, including the sun, why do we not experience that kind of dominion today? Theoretical physics posits that time and space are an illusion. Here is an example: If we imagine ourselves walking on a beach in California while we sit in our office in New York, we, in effect, make footprints in the sand before we even land in the sunshine state. Kabbalah agrees, and as the Zohar tells us, our thoughts create our reality. While sitting in our office during a snowstorm, if we imagine ourselves on the beach in Acapulco, are we really there in that thought? Absolutely. Can we feel the warmth of the sun and the sand beneath our feet? Absolutely. So what is reality? We have been so conditioned to what reality is that we are forgetting what reality is really all about. The physicist tells us that reality is not what the five senses observe or experience.

Thus we begin with the premise that what we imagine and what we think is reality. However, if we think we can produce a million dollars and want a million dollars to appear right now in front of us, why does it not appear? According to the physicist, what we see physically is not reality. The Zohar says that humankind was created with total control of every situation in life but there are conditions. First of all, we have to know with certainty that it could be so. For example, if the doctor informs us that the only thing he can promise is temporary relief, and if we believe what he says, in our mind we have then established only temporary relief, and that is thus all we will get. On the other hand, when we seek totality itself, then that is what we get.

Our consciousness is in control of what we will get but, unfortunately, because we are so consumed by the illusion, we never achieve that which we want to achieve. Yet we have this potential to control everything in the universe. Nothing moves in this universe without humankind's activity. We may perceive with our five senses that we are unsuccessful at stopping the sun, yet the fact that we do not observe the sun stopping does not necessarily mean that the sun has not stopped. The sun moving could be the illusion—and indeed this is so, for it is the earth that moves.

What we are talking about here is a cosmic code. As the Zohar explains, there is nothing in the Bible that can be understood or interpreted on a physical level. The Bible provides us with an understanding, not only of the cosmos but also of our own lives. The Bible provides the technology to reestablish the moment before the sin of Adam, when humanity was still in total control of reality. Therefore, if we can achieve the state of consciousness of Adam before the sin, and if we have learned the methodology of how to connect with the 99 Percent Reality, we can control physicality.

Kabbalah is a technology that explains how to make the connection to the 99 Percent Reality. For example, in the Ana Beko'ach prayer, which we recite in the morning and afternoon, there are meditations on particular Hebrew letters. Why did the *Sefer Yetzirah* ("Book of Formation") bring this to our attention? Why did the Zohar bring it to our attention? Why did Rav Isaac Luria (the Ari, 1534 – 1572) bring it to our attention? Why did all the kabbalists bring it to our attention? As Rav Shimon says, it is because in the Age of Aquarius, which is the time of the coming of the Messiah, all this information will be restored to us. It is here now and all in print. We just need to walk into a bookstore and buy it. No one can tell anyone they cannot study Kabbalah anymore. There is no longer any question regarding the availability of this information. Some may understand more and others may understand a little less but the wisdom is all here. When we pray, we meditate with consciousness because prayer is a system, a connection, a channel by which we can actually control and have dominion over the physical world of matter, over everything around us—despite the fact that we may not see it.

How do we bring out our potential? The wisdom of Kabbalah teaches us how to access the potential of Adam within the individual self by connecting with a reality that is beyond past, present, and future. We can have possession of something physical but this does not necessarily mean that we control it. When a kabbalist makes the connection, he or she does not need the manifestation of the physical entity to be able to make use of it. They make use of energies that are far superior to the physical connections.

This passage in the Zohar teaches us that whatever we desire is what we get. But the question is one of how to maintain our connection to it. For example, we could be thinking about one thing and a second later our mind drifts off to something else. We thought about it, and the next minute we lost it. There is constant interference in the 1 Percent Illusionary World that does not let us maintain this connection. Kabbalah explains how to maintain the connection. In the Study of the Ten Luminous Emanations we learn there is a method by which we can capture and maintain what it is that we desire. Abraham both captured it and knew how to maintain it.

2 And he lifted up his eyes and saw three men standing nearby. And when he saw them, he ran from the entrance of his tent to meet them and bowed himself to the ground. 3 And said, "My Lord, if I have found favor in your eyes, do not pass, I pray you, from your servant. 4 Let a little water, I pray you, be fetched, and wash your feet and rest yourselves under this tree.

Abraham and the Angels

When Abraham greeted the three angels, he offered only a small quantity of water. Since water is chesed—love from the Creator—it can either be shared with others, through thoughts and actions, or else given over to the dark side. Abraham was not sure if his guests would share the water—*chesed*—they received with others or give it to the dark side. This is a lesson for us about the spiritual nature of *chesed*. The Creator is careful about how much *chesed* we can receive from Him. If we have thoughts of sharing and giving to others, then we receive a greater quantity of *chesed*. But, on the other hand, if our thoughts are not about sharing and giving to others, then the *chesed* from the Creator will be shut off from us.

5 And I will fetch a morsel of bread and comfort your hearts; after that you will pass on, for you have come to your servant." And they said, "So do as you have said."

Vayera — the Most Significant Portion

Kabbalists refer to Vayera as the most significant portion. It is often compared to the Book of Shemot—the second of the Five Books of Moses, which deals with the plagues and the splitting of the Red Sea. The Zohar explains that the exodus was not an escape from Egypt. The Israelites had no intention of leaving a comfortable life there. The bondage referred to in the biblical story relates to their connection to physicality and the chaos, pain, and suffering that it brings.

Vayera, however, has more to do with the seed level. This is the reason it appears first—prior to the exodus from Egypt. That which is first is the seed, and that which follows is the tree. Kabbalists refer to Vayera as the most significant portion, and we shall soon find out why.

The Angels Heal Abraham

At the beginning of this chapter, God appeared to Abraham as he was sitting at the entrance of his tent, when three strangers approached. The first verse says that Abraham lifted up his eyes. This verse seems perplexing, and yet when the first verse is incomprehensible there is a great deal of Light to be revealed. Commentators insert the following interpretation of the actual words: Abraham could not offer his customary hospitality to strangers on this day because he was both ninety years old and also recovering from his circumcision. Therefore, God appeared before Abraham. We read further that Abraham saw three people—who are in fact three angels. Abraham did not know they were angels. He thought they were people to whom he could extend his natural generosity—despite the fact that this was the third day following his circumcision, and the third day is the most difficult. The Bible says Abraham asked the strangers not to pass him by. Here the Zohar engages in a lengthy discussion regarding the three angels and their mission: God sent the angels to attend to Abraham. Raphael, the angel of healing, came to heal him; Michael, the angel of *chesed* (mercy), blessed Abraham and Sarah to have a child; and Gabriel, the angel of judgment, was sent to destroy the cities of Sodom and Gomorrah—where evil had reached a level worse than anywhere else on Earth.

Letting Go of Ego

Can an angel be in different places at the same time? Yes. We are told that even though there may be a thousand circumcisions going on at the same time, Elijah is present at all of them. How can he be in a thousand places at once? Science is now beginning to discover some of the concepts that the kabbalists understood two thousand years ago. The "outlandish" ideas found in Kabbalah are now becoming a source of enlightenment for all of humankind, and not just a select few, as it was until recently.

The reality of time, space, and motion, experienced as part of this physical dimension, is merely an illusion. And the way to comprehend the nature of illusion is to give up the ego. The ego confines us to a prison of limitation, and thus of pain and suffering. When we are in the "me" consciousness our only option is to stay and embrace the pain, which is the result of our own actions. Why is the ego so important, and why did Rav Ashlag stress the significance of the ego in so much of his writing? It is because the consequences of dismissing the idea that we need to relinquish the ego are pain and suffering. It is a difficult choice to make, however, and it is left to each individual's discretion.

6 And Abraham hastened into the tent to Sarah and said, "Quick, make ready three measures of fine meal, knead it, and make cakes on the hearth." 7 And Abraham ran to the herd and fetched a good and tender calf and gave it to a young man, and he hurried to prepare it. 8 And he took butter, and milk, and the calf which he had prepared and set these before them. And he stood by them under the tree and they did eat. 9 And they asked him, "Where is your wife Sarah?" And he said, "There, in the tent." 10 And he said, "I will certainly return to you about this time next year, and Sarah your wife will have a son." And Sarah was listening at the entrance to the tent, which was behind him. 11 Now Abraham and Sarah were old and well stricken in age, and Sarah was past the age of childbearing. 12 Therefore, Sarah laughed to herself as she thought, "After I am waxed old will I have pleasure, my lord being old also?" 13 And the Lord said to Abraham, "Why did Sarah laugh and say, 'Will I surely have a child, now that I am old?' 14 Is anything too hard for the Lord? I will return to you at the appointed time next year and Sarah will have a son." 15 Then Sarah denied this for she was afraid, saying, "I did not laugh." And He said, "Yes, you did laugh." 16 And the men rose to leave, they looked down toward Sodom, and Abraham went with them to see them on their way.

The Meaning of Immortality

The lesson we learn from this section is that when miracles are concealed from manifesting in our lives we fall prey to the illusion of physical reality. However, we can override physical reality with certainty. I used to think that immortality meant no death but now I am beginning to understand that immortality means creating life from death.

Three Dots Above the Word *Elav*

In Beresheet 18:9 in the Torah Scroll, there are an additional three dots above the word *elav*, which means "to him." The Zohar explains that the three dots connect us to the three angels who came to visit Abraham. Although the third angel was the principal angel, come to give the message to Sarah that she would be blessed with a child, all three angels arrived with the same message.

The Zohar says that the angel who came to inform Sarah and Abraham about the birth of their child was practically a participant in the event of conception. At the age of 90, Sarah was informed by the angels that she would give birth, and when she heard this she laughed. However, the moment the angel revealed this message to her, her reproductive organs appeared, and her menstruation began. The moment the angel shared the message there was a physical manifestation.

What we can glean for ourselves from this portion is that energy forces known as "angels" are real and perform specific functions, and that there is a system by which we can call upon angels. However, this knowledge is not apparent to the general public. What we are trying to do by connecting with this section is to call on angels to avoid catastrophe. This reading gives us the opportunity to call upon angels for any purpose. The Zohar says that angels can either bring good tidings or the opposite. Why were there three angels? If Gabriel was sent to destroy Sodom and Gomorrah, why did he have to pass by Abraham?

Since we have the three dots in the text, and the merit to study Kabbalah, we have the ability to learn about the meaning of these dots. Everything in this universe is structured according to the Three Column System. There are three elements that make up the atom—which is why it is so powerful—Right (proton), Left (electron), and Central (neutron). We are made up of atoms—every cell contains some hundred trillion atoms.

Sarah was born without female organs; it was not in her DNA, and yet now she was going to have a baby all the same. According to the structure of our DNA, if a person loses an arm, although it seems there is currently no possibility of the limb being restored—yet a miracle can achieve such an apparent impossibility. In this instance, Sarah had no female organs to begin with. What we learn from this scripture then is that it appears to be possible to extract something out of nothing—so we can create something where nothing existed before. The three dots show us that this power is not found in splitting the atom but in the knowledge of this unique energy of the Three Column System. If there is a breakdown, we can still take control of every aspect of physicality—and this is God's gift to humankind. But most people cannot fathom such a possibility. Only in the spiritual discipline of Kabbalah is there an emphasis on the Three Column System and the importance of restriction. The three dots also refer to the three patriarchs: Abraham, Isaac, and Jacob. Abraham is the chariot for the Sefira of Chesed (sharing), while Isaac is the chariot for Gevurah (receiving), and thirdly Jacob—who will ultimately become manifested as the chariot for Tiferet (restriction) in this portion—is the balancing force between sharing and receiving.

This chapter illustrates the idea of the patriarchs—the manifesting forces—and the energy that they bring. A flood devastated the entire world during the time of Noah, yet through this portion we obtain a blessing that we can use today to restructure that which has gone awry, the way things do in a flood or any other disaster. Despite the effects of our past actions, if things are not going the way they should, we can access the positive Right Column. Let us never forget that we are the producer of the show and thus can put all of these elements together if we wish to. However, we cannot take advantage of it if we have done anything to disrupt the atoms that make up the world. This is not a question of who is right or wrong—if something of a negative nature emerges, it is always wrong. Suffering, pain, and uncertainty will never bring unity to this world. How then can we bring unity? Through this reading, we are given the chance. Our suffering is not God's punishment—it is an opportunity to correct a negative situation. With these three dots we have an opportunity to restore our consciousness and restructure it, freed from the distortions we have created.

The Three Column System and Anti-Matter

The Zohar indicates that the three angels in this chapter represent the Three Column System: Right, Left, and Central. In the Zohar, Rav Ashlag gives a lengthy explanation, and specific illustration about angels, referring to this section of the bible. He discusses how energy operates by restriction, by letting go of the ego—that when our egos have been touched, we should restrict and not react. Rav Ashlag gleaned from the Zohar that restriction creates anti-matter. The benefit to anti-matter is that it alone creates *Or deChasadim*, the Light of Mercy. The Right and Left Columns are constantly in conflict, each with the desire to engulf and envelop the other, until the Central Column—the act of restriction—motivates anti-matter and *incorporates*—but does not cut out—the negative pole, the Left

Column of the Desire to Receive. The Central Column includes and incorporates the Left and the Right Columns into this circular concept of energy. We cannot cut out any element of this circuitry and still have Light.

As was discussed previously, everything that exists in this world has the potential to incorporate the Three Column System. Only pure evil has no basis in sharing. There are people who exist in this world for no other reason than to cause pain and suffering. Where they come from is explained in the Zohar. Other than these few people, every form of energy, whether negative or positive, is an integral part of the whole energy system. Therefore, by restriction we arouse anti-matter and thereby incorporate the Left Column, which is necessary for this circuitry. Without a Left Column—the Desire to Receive—there is no energy. The three angels indicate that when we institute this Three Column System, we will have all the things these angels came for, namely healing, rescue from catastrophe, and the miracle of physical regeneration. Those who have the merit will understand this.

The journey begins for those who accept responsibility for their *tikkun* (spiritual correction) and for spreading the wisdom of Kabbalah. Letting go of ego and accepting responsibility are the prerequisites. This knowledge must be earned, and it guarantees a future that can be changed despite the heavy burden of prior incarnations. Everyone must undergo a certain *tikkun* but it can be transformed.

Transformation and the Resurrection of DNA

What is this section meant to reveal to us? Are we to understand that a man of 100 years and a woman of 90 years can have a child? Yes. It was a miracle. Both Abraham and Sarah achieved a tremendous transformation. Abraham resurrected his DNA or, as intimated in the Zohar, he received new DNA, not the same as that with which he was born. Humanity is still many years away from thinking about the notion that DNA can be changed. Perhaps the work we have done at the Kabbalah Centre has shortened this time-span.

When the angel told Abraham he was going to father a son, Sarah overheard and laughed. She could not understand that she could possibly give birth, nor how Abraham, who was 100 years old, could possibly bring forth the seed. The Zohar says that if we do not believe humanity has the power and the consciousness to overcome problems, we never will overcome them. Why would we not want to repair a missing or damaged limb or organ? We do not accept this as a possibility only because we do not want to be perceived as foolish. If we do not know that it can happen, it will never happen. Despite Abraham's personal strength, his efforts to transform himself from 100 years old to 20 years old would not have succeeded if he did not know it was possible. This section tells us that it is possible. We are not destined to be the bedfellows of pain, suffering, and helplessness. And yet we have parted ways from the Bible so drastically because its stories seem so ridiculous to us that we have deemed it meaningless—even to the point where reading scripture makes no sense.

17 And the Lord said, "Shall I hide from Abraham what I am about to do? 18 Seeing that Abraham will surely become a great and mighty nation and all nations on Earth will be blessed through him. 19 For I know him, that he will command his children and his household after him and they will keep the way of the Lord by doing what is right and just, that the Lord will bring about for Abraham what He has spoken to him." 20 And the Lord said, "Because the cry of Sodom and Gomorrah is great and their sin so grievous, 21 I will go down now and see if what they have done is as bad as the outcry that has come to me. And if not, I will know." 22 And the men turned their faces away and went toward Sodom, but Abraham remained standing before the Lord. 23 And Abraham drew near and said: "Will You destroy the righteous with the wicked? 24 What if there are fifty righteous people in the city? Will You really destroy it and not spare the place for the sake of the fifty righteous people in it? 25 Far be it from You to do such a thing— to slay the righteous with the wicked; and treating the righteous as if they are wicked. Far be it from You: Will not the Judge of all the Earth do right?" 26 And the Lord said, "If I find fifty righteous people in the city of Sodom, I will spare the whole place for their sake." 27 And Abraham answered: "See now that I have taken upon me to speak to the Lord, though I am nothing but dust and ashes, 28 what if the number of the righteous is five

less than fifty? Will You destroy the whole city because of five people?" And He said, "If I find forty-five there, I will not destroy it." 29 And he spoke to Him yet again and said, "What if only forty are found there?" And He said, "I will not do it, for the sake of forty." 30 And he said to Him, "Let not the Lord be angry, and I will speak. What if only thirty can be found there?" And He answered, "I will not do it if I find thirty there." 31 And he said, "See now that I have taken upon me to speak to the Lord, what if only twenty can be found there?" And He said, "I will not destroy it, for the sake of twenty." 32 And he said, "Let not the Lord be angry, and I will speak yet just this once: What if only ten can be found there?" And He answered, "I will not destroy it, for the sake of ten." 33 And the Lord went His way once He finished speaking with Abraham, and Abraham returned to his place.

Beresheet 19:1 And two angels came to Sodom in the evening, and Lot sat on the gate of Sodom: And Lot, seeing them, rose to meet them and bowed down with his face towards the ground. 2 And he said, "See now, my lords, turn aside, I pray you, to your servant's house and tarry all night. And wash your feet and then go on your way early in the morning." And they said, "No, we will spend the night in the street." 3 And he pressed upon them greatly; that they did go with him and entered his house. And he

made them a feast and baked unleavened bread, and they ate.

Evil and Teleportation

Two angels, disguised as humans, came to Sodom and Gomorrah, one for the purpose of saving Lot, and one for the purpose of destroying the evil people of these two cities. An evil person is someone who desires to only see evil, pain, and suffering in other people. Such people have the evil eye. Do they benefit from the evil eye? No. They gain nothing. An evil person has no other function other than to dispense their evil energy.

The Zohar tells us that the day before the two angels arrived, one of Lot's daughters was killed by the evil people of the city because she was caught committing an act of kindness—offering a poor man something to eat. Lot welcomed the two people, the angels, into his home, despite what had happened to his daughter a day earlier. In describing this section, the Zohar introduces us to the idea of teleportation. Abraham came to his nephew, Lot—who was hundreds of miles away—by means of teleportation, and told him not to fear but to trust and take the visitors into his house. Lot trusted his uncle and invited them in.

Teleportation is one of the concepts we, at the Kabbalah Centres, teach that people call outlandish. But, as I have said repeatedly, if we as a generation have earned the merit to study the Wisdom of Kabbalah, then we will also be witness to the mastering of so-called outlandish practices. This story is presented to impress upon us that teleportation is something very possible and very real. And this portion gives us the opportunity to seek this level of consciousness. In following the spiritual rules of the game of life, we can obtain this energy and level of consciousness. The most difficult aspect of human nature is that we must overcome our own ego, no matter what station in life we occupy.

4 But before they had gone to bed, the men of the city of Sodom surrounded the house—both young and old—all the people from every quarter. 5 And they called to Lot and said to him, "Where are the men who came to you tonight? Bring them out to us so that we may know them." 6 And Lot went outside to meet them and shut the door behind him, 7 and said, "I pray you, brothers, do not do this wicked thing. 8 See now, I have two daughters who have not known man. Let me, I pray you, bring them out to you, and you can do to them what is good in your eyes, but to these men do nothing, for they have come under the shadow of my roof." 9 And they said, "Stand back." And they said, "This one fellow came here to sojourn, and now he wants to be a judge. Now we will treat you worse than them." They kept pressing against the man Lot, and moved near to break the door. 10 But the men inside reached out and pulled Lot back into the house and shut the door. 11 And they smote the men who were at the door of the house, both great and small, with blindness so that they wearied themselves to find the door. 12 And the men said to Lot, "Do you have anyone else here—sons-in-law, sons or daughters, or anyone else in the city who belongs to you? Get them out of this place, 13 for we are going to destroy this place because the outcry of them is waxen great before the face of the Lord and the Lord has sent us to destroy it." 14 And Lot went out

and spoke to his sons-in-law, who married his daughters, and said, "Hurry and get out of this place, because the Lord is about to destroy this city!" But his sons-in-law thought he was joking.

The Power of Charity

The story of Sodom and Gomorrah appears to be absurd. Abraham's nephew, Lot, found it worthwhile to dwell in a place where the most evil people in the world lived. In this community, it was the law that anyone who participated in any form of sharing was put to death. When the two angels came into town, Lot offered them hospitality, which he learned from his uncle, Abraham. As soon as the dwellers in the city heard he had extended hospitality, they pounded on his door and demanded that the guests be delivered to them. He refused and offered his two daughters instead, saying "Don't touch these strangers."

Lot was living in a den, not of thieves but of murderers. Was Lot a *tzadik* (righteous person)? The Zohar tells us that, a day earlier, Lot's daughter had given food to a hungry man, and when the townspeople found out they took his daughter to the roof, bound her, poured honey over her entire body, and left her to be eaten alive by bees. Lot chose to live among these evil people, and thereby he risked his own life and the lives of his family by offering hospitality to the strangers. Why did he do this after what he had gone through with his own daughter just one day before? It does not make sense. Is this story here to teach us he was such a charitable man that he preferred to live in such a wicked community? No. This section teaches us that the literal story is to be dismissed. Instead it shows us the power of extending charity—the power that saved Lot is the power of *chesed* (loving kindness). The story teaches us that the opportunity to share is always accompanied by an inconvenience, by a very good reason not to share.

15 And when the morning dawned, the angels urged Lot, saying, "Arise! Take your wife and your two daughters who are here, or you will be consumed in the iniquity of the city." 16 And while he lingered, the men grasped his hand and the hands of his wife and of his two daughters and led them safely out of the city, for the Lord was merciful to them. 17 And it came to pass when they had brought them out, that He said, "Flee for your life, do not look back, and don't stop anywhere in the plain, escape to the mountains or you will be swept away!" 18 And Lot said to them, "No, my lords, please! 19 See now, your servant has found favor in your eyes, and you have shown great kindness to me in saving my life. But I can't flee to the mountains, lest some evil take me and I die. 20 Look, here is a town near enough to run to, and it is small. Let me flee to it—it is very small, isn't it, and my soul will live." 21 And He said to him, "Very well, I will grant this request too; I will not overthrow the city you speak of. 22 But flee there quickly, because I cannot do anything until you reach it." That is why the city was called Zo'ar.

The Angels' Purpose

Vayera provides us with an opportunity to remove much of the chaos that rules over our lives. The reading of the Torah Scroll on Shabbat is the channel for the Lightforce of God to be revealed in this universe. The three angels who came to visit Abraham in this story were not protective entities but rather transmitters of the Lightforce of God—bearers who possesses the ultimate energy to remove chaos. What warranted these three appearing? The angel Raphael, who came to heal Abraham, also came to save Lot from the destruction that was to take place in the evil towns of Sodom and Gomorrah. An angel, in general, does not have the ability to be in touch with two separate aspects of the Lightforce of God at the same time. Their structure—the way they are created with the Hebrew letters—limits them to one function. However, in Vayera, it appears as if the angel Raphael had two functions—healing and saving. This story gives us the opportunity to receive both healing as well as the injection of extraordinary levels of the Lightforce of God with which to annihilate evil. From what we read it was seemingly impossible for Lot and his family to survive since the entire town was destined to be buried. Yet Lot and his family were saved. In this portion, healing and saving are one and the same, thus the angel Raphael was essentially taking on one mission.

Although we have the opportunity to receive all of these beneficent tools from the Creator to assist us—like the *Mem, Hei, Shin*, like the reading of the Torah—it does not address the original cause that led to our needing them. If we are in a situation from which we cannot extricate ourselves, like Lot and his family, we need to realize that the reason we are there in the first place is because there is something for which we have not taken responsibility. This is not a concept that is easily accepted. Humanity has a history of abdicating responsibility after a tragedy. We know how to market ourselves as victims, and yet misfortunes do not happen by themselves. We do not necessarily assume responsibility, which is a precondition for eliminating chaos.

We know that trees grow as part of the natural order of things. And we also believe that chaos is something natural and beyond our influence or our participation in it. This is very far from the truth.

The beneficence these angels represent indicates that a being like Abraham, the essence of *chesed*, is the real precondition for human life. If we do not meet the standards of Abraham, then whatever action we perform will result in chaos. Even when we are in the abyss of chaos with no way out, the Lightforce of God, experienced as the angel, can take us out.

Lot was saved because of his own merit—the Lightforce of God saved Lot and his family before the overturning of the cities of Sodom and Gomorrah. The angel of Abraham came to Lot at that moment in time and told him that unless one is in a state of constant sharing one cannot expect miracles nor can one expect that the negativity, which comes in the form of illness or chaos, can ever be removed. This is a universal law. From the moment that Lot spoke to Abraham, he took on the personal responsibility to share without the intention of being saved. Although he lacked in the nature of sharing, which is why he chose to live in a wicked place, he now assumed this responsibility. The spirit of Abraham is what we must come to live with. When we share for the sake of sharing, not for what we can receive in return—and we leave the outcome to the Light, knowing the Light will ultimately act for us—the Light must respond.

Abraham had no evil eye. He did not reflect on what he needed or what he wanted; he knew the laws of the universe. This is the way Abraham lived; and this is the way we will merit what is truly ours. What detaches this protective shield, and destroys what is around us, is our own envy. If we see ourselves as victims, for whatever reason, and claim that someone has perpetrated evil upon us, we are not a vessel for receiving this awesome degree of the Lightforce of God. We are constantly subjected to media telling us that getting and possessing is of the ultimate importance. The messages we receive are not about sharing with others. At the Kabbalah Centres, we are not part of this messaging. The universal laws do not operate on me first and you second. When we maintain the intention to share without commingling it with the notion of satisfying our own needs, we can ultimately fulfill the needs of all humanity.

23 By the time Lot reached Zo'ar, the sun had risen over the land. 24 Then the Lord rained down brimstone and fire on Sodom and Gomorrah—from the Lord out of Heaven. 25 And he overthrew those cities and the entire plain, including all the inhabitants of the cities and that which grew upon the ground. 26 But his wife looked back, and she became a pillar of salt.

Destroying Negativity

Lot was not a righteous person. The Creator's decree was to overturn the entire city, to literally turn it upside down and remove every trace of its existence. Why not just kill all of the inhabitants and let the land remain? This is the intensity of the negative energy that the people of Sodom and Gomorrah generated.

The only time in history when we came close to such a situation occurred in Spain. The hatred towards the Jewish people was so intense that, to this day, many traces of Jewish existence have been expunged from Spain's history. This is the equivalent of the land being turned upside down. Even in Germany, the Satan left some synagogues standing; and some remnant of the Jewish population still remains there to this day. This is not the case in Spain. When this type of destruction occurs, it is so irrational and so inexplicable that it forces us to examine something that is very uncomfortable for us to consider, and of course we do not have to accept it—but is it just possible that maybe the responsibility lies within us?

The Nature of Conflict

The angel instructed Lot to take his family and flee the city of Gomorrah and not to look back. Lot's wife did not listen; she turned around and became a pillar of salt. What are we to learn from this? The Zohar says the answer is that it is in our power to make things occur that we believe cannot happen. That which has been destroyed, for whatever reason, has been put into a state of disunity.

Do not think that conflict only happens on the physical level, which is the lowest level of confrontation. An argument is not merely an exchange of ideas. To learn how to overcome disaster, we have to learn the manner in which to confront. We have to learn what truth is and what it is not. If we have an opinion, we need to voice it, and to live our lives accordingly. However, this does not give us or anyone the right to coerce another person. We can sometimes feel so strongly about certain beliefs that we do more harm than those people who imposed laws against generosity. A society that tells us how we should live can set people at each other's throats merely by the strengthening of their respective beliefs. Violent conflict, even for all the right reasons, will never provide tranquility or contentment. How does the Light remove darkness? The Zohar says no matter how right we are, restriction is how the Light reveals itself in darkness. It is the same with the filament in a light bulb, which represents the element of restriction.

Connecting with this reading gives us protection against being in the wrong place at the wrong time.

The Corruption of Jealousy and Envy

It is written that the cities of Sodom and Gomorrah were turned upside down; the earth below came to be above and completely buried the cities and the surrounding area. What are we to understand from the wording here? Why were the cities not destroyed by a natural disaster, a flood or fire? The turning of reality upside down is its own kind of disaster. What happened in Sodom and Gomorrah will happen in our time. The energy of *Oy* (Woe) and *Ashrei* (Blessing) will manifest to the extreme. Then there will be no room for negativity of any kind—not a little bit of jealousy, not a smidgen of envy, not a morsel of hate. There will be no trace of any of these things. Jealousy is jealousy, envy is envy, and hate is hate, no matter to what degree we are engaged in such feelings. We will not be judged by the amount of jealousy we display, but whether we have been jealous at all. It does not matter whether we steal five dollars or five million, the action of stealing is the same—so we cannot afford any negative behavior.

27 And Abraham got up early in the morning and returned to the place where he had stood before the Lord. 28 And he looked toward Sodom and Gomorrah, and toward all the land of the plain, and he saw smoke rising from the country, like smoke from a furnace. 29 And it came to pass when God destroyed the cities of the plain that God remembered Abraham, and he sent Lot out of the midst of the overthrow, when He overthrew the cities in which Lot had dwelt. 30 And Lot and his two daughters left Zo'ar and dwelt in the mountains, for he was afraid to stay in Zo'ar. He and his two daughters dwelt in a cave. 31 And the firstborn daughter said to the younger, "Our father is old, and there is no man on Earth to come lie with us, as is the manner all over the Earth. 32 Come, let us make our father drink wine and we will lie with him, that we may preserve the seed of our father." 33 And they made their father drink wine that night, and the firstborn went in and lay with her father, and he was not aware of when she lay down or when she got up. 34 And it came to pass on the next day the firstborn said to the younger, "See, last night I lay with my father. Let us make him drink wine again tonight, and you go in and lie with him so we can preserve the seed of our father." 35 And they made their father to drink wine that night also, and the younger daughter went and lay with him and he was not aware of when she lay down or when she got up. 36 Thus both of Lot's daughters were

with child by their father. 37 And the firstborn had a son, and she named him Moab; he is the father of the Moabites unto this day. 38 The younger daughter also had a son, and she named him Ben-Ami; he is the father of the Ammonites unto this day.

The Birth of Messiah

This section encapsulates the energy of *Mashiach* (the Messiah). Here we read about the daughters of Lot sleeping with their father, and in the Torah there is a dot above the Hebrew word *uvekuma*, which means "when she rose," referring to Lot's older daughter rising after she had sexual relations with her father. The Zohar explains that the dot above this word indicates that there was assistance from the Light of the Creator in this act—which will ultimately result in the birth of the Messiah. Within this story is the seed of *Mashiach*, and thus we can connect to this energy that enables us to remove chaos from our lives and the world. What are we to learn from this dot, especially in a story about incest? Ruth came from the nation of Moab, and she was the great grandmother of King David, and *Mashiach* descends from King David. This reveals to us that the highest state of consciousness seems to be born from the most unholy of unions—sometimes the vessel is covered with dirt so Satan will leave it alone.

Another layer of meaning we understand from the insertion of this dot is that, like the dot, we must all strive to make ourselves small, with less ego—and by this I mean it is not for us to judge anyone. If *Mashiach* can come from incest, then who are we to judge the actions of others? The dot gives us the energy to look inwardly at ourselves and to stop judging other people. Moreover, if an incestuous relationship can result in the Messiah, this indicates that painful, negative energy can be transformed and become the seed of the most wonderful energy.

Beresheet 20:1 And Abraham journeyed from there toward the south country and for a while stayed in Gerar before dwelling between Kadesh and Shur. 2 And Abraham said of his wife Sarah, "She is my sister." Then Abimelech, king of Gerar, sent and took Sarah. 3 But God came to Abimelech in a dream one night and said to him, "Behold you are a dead man, for the woman you have taken; she is a man's wife." 4 But Abimelech had not gone near her, so he said, "Lord, will you slay an innocent nation? 5 Did he not say to me, 'She is my sister,' and she even said, 'He is my brother.' In the integrity of my heart and innocence of my hand have I done this." 6 And God said to him in the dream, "Yes, I know you did this with integrity in your heart, and so I have kept you from sinning against me. That is why I did not let you touch her. 7 Now return the man's wife, for he is a prophet, and he will pray for you and you will live. But if you do not return her, you may be sure that you and all that is yours will die." 8 Therefore Abimelech rose early in the morning and summoned all his servants, and when he told them all that had happened, they were very much afraid. 9 Then Abimelech called Abraham and said, "What have you done to us? How have I offended you that you have brought such great sin upon me and my kingdom? You have done things to me that should not be done." 10 And Abimelech asked Abraham, "What was your reason for doing this?"

11 Abraham replied, "Because I thought that there surely is no fear of God in this place, and they will kill me because of my wife. 12 Besides, she is indeed my sister, she is the daughter of my father but not the daughter of my mother; and she became my wife. 13 And it came to pass, when God caused me to wander from my father's household, that I said to her, 'This is how you can show your love to me: Everywhere we go, say of me, 'He is my brother.' " 14 And Abimelech brought sheep and oxen and menservants and women servants and gave them to Abraham, and he returned Sarah his wife to him. 15 And Abimelech said, "See, my land is before you; live wherever you like." 16 And to Sarah he said, "See, I have given your brother a thousand pieces of silver. This is to cover the offense against you before all who are with you; you are completely reproved." 17 So Abraham prayed to God, and God healed Abimelech, his wife, and his maidservants so that they could bear children. 18 For the Lord had closed up every womb in Abimelech's household because of Abraham's wife Sarah.

Beresheet 21:1 And the Lord visited Sarah as He had said, and the Lord did for Sarah what He had promised. 2 For Sarah conceived and bore a son to Abraham in his old age, at the very time God had promised him. 3 And Abraham gave the name Isaac to the son Sarah bore him. 4 And Abraham circumcised his son Isaac when he was eight days old, as

God commanded him. 5 And Abraham was a hundred years old when his son Isaac was born to him. 6 And Sarah said, "God has brought me laughter, and everyone who hears will laugh with me." 7 And she said, "Who would have said to Abraham that Sarah would nurse children, for I have borne him a son in his old age?" 8 And the child grew and was weaned, and Abraham made a great feast on the day that Isaac was weaned.

Vessel for the Light

In this reading, with the birth of Isaac, we have an opportunity to create the vessel we need to draw the Lightforce of God.

9 And Sarah saw the son that Hagar the Egyptian had borne to Abraham was mocking. 10 And she said to Abraham, "Cast out this bondwoman and her son, for the son of this bondwoman will not be heir with my son, with Isaac." 11 And the thing distressed Abraham greatly because it concerned his son. 12 And God said to Abraham, "Do not be so distressed about the boy and your bondwoman. Listen to whatever Sarah tells you, because it is through Isaac that your seed will be called. 13 And also of the son of the bondwoman will I make a nation, because he is your seed." 14 And Abraham rose early the next morning and took bread and a bottle of water and gave them to Hagar, putting them on her shoulders and then sent her away with the boy. And she wandered in the wilderness of Beersheba. 15 And when the water in the bottle was gone, she put the boy under one of the bushes. 16 And she went a good way off and sat down, about a bowshot away, for she said, "Let me not see the death of the child. And she sat over against him and lifted her voice and wept. 17 And God heard the voice of the lad, and the angel of God called to Hagar from Heaven and said to her, "What is the matter, Hagar? Do not be afraid; God has heard the lad crying as he lies there. 18 Arise, lift the lad up and take him by the hand, for I will make him a great nation." 19 And God opened her eyes and she saw a well of water, and she went and filled the bottle with water and gave the lad to drink.

20 And God was with the lad, and he grew and dwelt in the wilderness and became an archer. 21 While he was living in the Desert of Paran, his mother got a wife for him from Egypt. 22 And it came to pass at that time that Abimelech and Phichol, the chief captain of his host, spoke to Abraham, saying, "God is with you in all that you do. 23 Now swear to me here before God that you will not deal falsely with me or with my son or with my son's son; but according to the kindness that I have shown you, you will do to me and to the land where you have sojourned." 24 And Abraham said, "I will swear." 25 And Abraham reproved Abimelech about a well of water that Abimelech's servants had violently taken away. 26 And Abimelech said, "I don't know who has done this. You did not tell me, and I heard about it only today." 27 And Abraham took sheep and oxen and gave them to Abimelech, and both of them made a covenant (treaty). 28 And Abraham set seven ewe lambs from the flock by themselves. 29 And Abimelech asked Abraham, "What is the meaning of these seven ewe lambs you have set by themselves?" 30 And he replied, "Accept these seven lambs from my hand as a witness that I dug this well." 31 So he called that place Beersheba, because there they both swore an oath. 32 After the treaty had been made at Beersheba, Abimelech and Phicol, the chief captain of his host, returned to the land of the Philistines. 33 And Abraham planted a grove in Beersheba, and

there he called upon the name of the Lord, the Eternal God. 34 And Abraham stayed in the land of the Philistines for many days.

Pollution and Water

Abraham was imbued with the energy of Right Column because he is the chariot of the Sefira of Chesed, which manifests physically as water. Water is our problem, and water is our solution. As far back as 1912, there was a concern that there was no water to replace the polluted water within us. Environmentally too, our water is polluted, and not because of insecticides or the fallout from nuclear explosions. Of course these pollutants do have a bearing on our water quality but they represent less than one percent of the problem. In the physical world, chesed is accompanied by pollution. Satan exists in this dimension in a non-physical form that has to be eliminated.

Beresheet 22:1 And it came to pass after these things that God tested Abraham. He said to him, "Abraham!" And he replied, "Here I am." 2 And God said, "Take your son, your only son, Isaac, whom you love, and go to the land of Moriah and offer him there for a burnt offering upon one of the mountains that I will tell you." 3 And Abraham rose early in the morning, and saddled his donkey and took two of his servants with him and his son Isaac, and cut the wood for the burnt offering; and rose up and went to the place of which God had told him. 4 Then on the third day Abraham lifted up his eyes and saw the place in the distance. 5 And Abraham said to his servants, "Stay here with the donkey while I and the boy go over there and worship, and then we will come back to you." 6 And Abraham took the wood for the burnt offering and placed it on his son Isaac, and he himself carried the fire and the knife, and they went on together. 7 And Isaac spoke to his father Abraham and said, "My father?" And he replied, "Yes, my son?" And he said, "See, the fire and wood are here, but where is the lamb for the burnt offering?" 8 And Abraham answered, "God Himself will provide the lamb for the burnt offering, my son." So they went on together. 9 And they reached the place God had told him about, and Abraham built an altar there and laid the wood on it, and he bound Isaac, his son, and laid him on the altar, on top of the wood. 10 And Abraham reached out his hand and

took the knife to slay his son. 11 And the angel of the Lord called out to him from Heaven, "Abraham! Abraham!" And he replied, "Here I am." 12 And he said, "Do not lay a hand on the boy, do not do anything to him, for now I know that you fear God, because you have not withheld from Me your son, your only son." 13 And Abraham lifted up his eyes and looked, and there in a thicket behind him he saw a ram caught by its horns. And Abraham went and took the ram and sacrificed it as a burnt offering instead of his son.

The Meaning of Sacrifice

The Binding of Isaac is the binding of selfish thoughts so we can think only about what we can do for someone else. It is to always connect our thoughts to the Tree of Good, while running away from any thoughts connected with the Tree of Evil—thoughts that do not involve the wellbeing of others—thereby setting our consciousness to remember the miracles.

The purpose of Kabbalah is to restore this true reality and bring us back to being fully human. Kabbalah is for elevating our subhuman nature, which can be even worse than the animal one.

The Sacrifice of Isaac: An Unlikely Story

We have within Vayera an incredible but perplexing story that I love so much. It is a narrative that those involved in or interested in the Bible have believed for 3,400 years. What could be more nonsensical than Abraham and Sarah being granted by the grace of God a child in their old age, only to be told by God to sacrifice that same child? A great deal of grief has resulted from accepting the stories in the Bible blindly. Are we to suppose that Abraham, a 137-year-old man, was able to bind his 37-year-old son so Isaac could not run away? The story makes no sense. Yet the very same Bible contains profound secrets concerning how to remove chaos from our lives. Those believers in the Bible who have for 3,400 years swayed the Jewish people and the whole world into concealing the Zohar, prefer the conventional interpretation of this story. However, we should not accept a story that is so incomprehensible and confounding.

How could anyone believe that a parent would willingly bring their child to be a sacrifice? This is not what the Bible means, though. Do not think that God needs appeasement in the form of slaughtering a child to curb His wrath upon His people. This is the story of the Right Column fighting the Left Column or the evil inclination, which is why it is called the Binding of Isaac.

These three stories in Vayera—Abraham's circumcision, Abraham and Sarah becoming fertile, and the Binding of Isaac—are all connected to each other and are not separate incidents. There is a message here: We are created with the ability to control our environment. However, since we do not believe in the possibility of humankind's dominion over our environment, there is nowhere in this world that such control exists. Those who can accept the power of mind over matter are reminded in these sections of the different structures of connection that were put into the universe so we can succeed in controlling our environment.

Destruction in the Name of God

Is murder permitted when, supposedly, God endorses it? Holy
war is a concept now, unfortunately, very familiar to our society.
Here, God instructed Abraham to slaughter his child in the Name
of God—and this is from the Holy Bible! Is the Bible saying that
in the Name of God everything is permitted? Of course this kind
of thinking is false. The literal translation of this chapter has been
so corrupted that it has brought upon us, not the wrath of God
but the wrath of Satan. We perpetrate the very violations that are
committed against us. We have become so adept at making excuses
that we have become the victim. Do we examine the abominations
and tragedies of the world? Do we question why they happen?

In my opinion, Abraham was the subject of an ugly fiction. He
was never prepared to sacrifice his son. The Zohar says that the
story is meant to teach us that we have a companion to be aware
of always—one that causes us to react. Negativity is part of the
package of being human, and this is why we have the Ana Beko'ach.
The message to be gleaned is not that Abraham was fully prepared
to slaughter his child as a sacrifice. Rather it is to instruct us that
each of us possesses the Desire to Receive, and what we have to
do is bind it, so that it does not have dominion. This is why the
section is named the Binding of Isaac. The only way the Desire
to Receive can be bound is to have more Right Column than Left
Column energy. This may sound simple in theory but it is not
simple in practice—it is a constant struggle. Nevertheless, it is the
methodology to aid the dominion of the Right Column, which will
restore everything in the universe back to what it should be and
bring humankind to a new consciousness—to a new DNA. When
this takes place, the Left Column will then come under our control.
When we bind our Desire for the Self Alone with the consciousness
of Sharing, by unifying the energy of the Right Column and the

Left Column, it can give us mastery over the energy of death. This Binding is the formula for removing all chaos.

The Purpose of the Bible: The Light's Manifestation

Would anyone take their son to be slaughtered? I would not want to be part of such a religion. Is anyone "holy" enough to obey God and sacrifice their child because it is His will? For 4,000 years, Kabbalah has suggested that the conventional perception of this story is a total distortion. We cannot accept this as a literal event. We should never forget that, although we tend to become a little holy and self-righteous, the Bible was never meant to be a tool for religious service or worship. We do not gather to pray to God so that He will shower His mercy upon us. If we think in this way then we must also conclude that He has done a poor job of that for the last 2,000 years. I am not referring to genocide past or present, I am referring to the daily cares and physical sufferings that each person experiences. It is impossible to escape the statistics. Millions of people suffer daily from the ravages of disease. Thus we come to the Centres to experience Shabbat, the only day in which we can draw the Light into our bodies and souls.

Certainly the conventional view of this story—that it could be "noble" to sacrifice one's own child—is difficult and confusing enough to warrant the effort and time required to read the Zohar, where it discusses this section of the Bible. As the Zohar reminds us, the words of the Bible are merely a way for the Lightforce of God to become manifest. What are we but our consciousness? For are we not guilty of sacrificing our children? I hear parents say that they work day and night for their children, not for themselves. At the same time, I also hear children say that all they want is for their parents to be home with them as much as possible. What the Bible is speaking about here is that we must bind our Desire to Receive—and it is going to require restriction on our part. The miracles of restriction are more incredible than one could ever dream of.

Binding Our Negativity

Abraham took Isaac to Mount Moriah, the place where the Temple would one day be built. He took along wood, as well as the rope that would bind Isaac, and the knife with which to slaughter him. The Zohar says that Abraham was not told to sacrifice Isaac—which is the reason that the portion is called the *Akedah* (Binding) of Isaac, to inform us that we must bind the Left Column, we must bind our negativity. This 4,000-year-old story is here to teach us that there is a system in place that allows the transformation of negative energy. Negative energy must be transformed, not destroyed or removed. Oncologists consider the cutting out of cancer to be effective if they can remove 99.9999 percent of it. But considering there are billions of cancer cells, there is still the likelihood that a hundred million are left inside a patient.

If we do not have the awareness that negativity must be transformed, we will not win the battle. This knowledge and understanding is what we, at the Kabbalah Centres, strive to share with the world. So when we connect to the story of the Binding of Isaac, we are not concentrating on the offering of Isaac—the only son of Sarah by Abraham as a sacrifice—instead we have an opportunity to listen to the Torah, which is the dispensation of the incredible knowledge by which we may improve our lives, and we should share this Light with all people of the world.

Observance of God?

Some commentators say that this story signifies the ultimate obedience to God. What kind of loving God asks this of his obedient servants? Why do we not question this? The Zohar raises this question and concludes that since God is solely a positive force, it is, therefore, not in the nature of God to request something negative. Yet the work we at The Kabbalah Centre are doing, to bring some sanity and purpose to what the Bible has to say, has been criticized by religious authorities.

Are we really to accept that Abraham, a man of 137, tied up a man of 37 with a cord to prevent his escape, and that Isaac obeyed his father and agreed to have his throat slit? Was Isaac meant to be bound and sacrificed on the very land where the Temple would be built? No. Written more than 2,000 years ago, the Zohar provides us with the concept of the Three Column System, which, in turn, teaches us about the atom and explains that this is, in fact, what the Bible has been trying to tell us with this story for the past 3,400 years. However, humans have always intervened and taken something that can operate in a structured, harmonious way, like the atom, and created with it an atom bomb—thus preventing the establishment of the Three Column System, which originates with Abraham.

Abraham embodies Chesed, *Or deChasadim* (Light of Mercy), which I call anti-matter. All chaos comes in the form of matter. *Or deChasadim*, anti-matter, removes chaos. When Abraham, who is *Or deChasadim*, binds the Left Column, we are being shown how anti-matter removes the negative aspect. When matter is not bound, it prevents the flow of Light through the universe and creates limitations such as time, space, and motion. While we might not understand it, the Binding of Isaac was not intended to be a blood sacrifice; it served to make a cohesive bond of the elements of this universe that are not bonded because of our greater expression of negativity. Our negativity is what brings about the destruction of the normal pattern of this structure because we do not function as Abraham did. We have the opportunity with this biblical portion to receive this energy of healing, rebirth, and the removal of chaos.

What Abraham did was a righteous act. When Abraham took his son, Isaac, to be slaughtered (bound), the Bible says that Rebecca was born. Isaac had reached a certain level of spiritual elevation—only when the binding of negativity took place was he elevated to reach the level of his soulmate. So who was really being tested, was it Abraham or Isaac? We should know that it is in the hands of all of us. Isaac was born with a level of Judgment; he had so much power. He was also the only one who stayed in Israel and did not leave.

14 And Abraham called that place Adonai-jireh, as it is said to this day, "On the mountain of the Lord it will be seen." 15 And the angel of the Lord called to Abraham from Heaven a second time, 16 and said, "By Myself I have sworn," said the Lord, "that because you have done this thing and have not withheld your son, your only son, 17 that in blessing I will bless you and I will multiply your seed as numerous as the stars of the Heaven and as the sand on the seashore. And your seed will possess the gates of his enemies, 18 and through your seed will all nations on Earth be blessed, because you have obeyed My voice." 19 So Abraham returned to his servants, and they rose and went together to Beersheba. And Abraham dwelt in Beersheba. 20 And it came to pass after these things that it was told to Abraham saying, "See, Milcah is also a mother; she has borne children to your brother Nahor: 21 Huz, the firstborn, and Buz, his brother, and Kemuel, the father of Aram, 22 And Chesed, and Hazo, and Pildash, and Jidlaph and Bethuel." 23 And Bethuel became the father of Rebecca. Milcah bore these eight sons to Abraham's brother Nahor. 24 And his concubine, whose name was Reumah, also had Tebah, and Gaham, and Tahash, and Maachah.

About the Haftarah

The Haftarah we read after the portion of Vayera is different for those of Ashkenazi descent and those of Sephardi descent. The Sephardim only read the first section that gives us the story of the wife of one of the sons of the prophets, who went to Elisha and asked for help. Since the time of her husband's passing, she did not know how to feed her children. Elisha asked what she had in the house. She replied that she had only a pot of oil. He instructed her to borrow vessels from all her neighbors and, behind closed doors, put oil in all of the pots she had thus obtained. She was able to fill all of the vessels with oil, and when there were no more empty vessels, the oil stopped flowing. She then sold the oil, paid her debt, and was able to live on the remainder.

Then the Haftarah discusses a Shunamite woman who invited Elisha into her house whenever he travelled through her town. When he asked her what he could do for her in return for her generosity, she replied that she did not require any assistance. He asked his servant about the woman and the servant told him that she did not have a son and that her husband was old. Elisha then prophesied that she would have a son within in the year. She did give birth to a son that year, but the young boy soon after died. The woman refused to accept her son's death, and she went to see Elisha, without telling her husband what had happened to the boy.

The Sephardim stop the story here. Ashkenazi communities continue to where the story has Elisha going to her house and reviving the child. The Sephardim stop before the end of this story because they did not want people to fixate on the story of the resurrection of the child. The fact that this woman believed the child could be and should be revived is what is important, not how he was revived. If we have the certainty, it can be so. The reason this woman did not tell her husband that her son had died was because she knew he would have doubted that resurrecting his son was possible, and his doubt would undermine the miracle, preventing it from happening.

BOOK OF BERESHEET:

Portion of Chayei Sarah

PORTION OF CHAYEI SARAH

Beresheet 23:1 And Sarah was one hundred, twenty and seven years old. These were the years of the life of Sarah. 2 And Sarah died at Kiriath Arba, that is Hebron in the land of Canaan, and Abraham went to mourn for Sarah and to weep for her.

The Life of Sarah and the Tree of Life

The Zohar and the commentators remark on how Sarah's age is presented in the Bible. It does not say 127 years; instead it says "one hundred, twenty and seven years." Why is the number seven presented as a plural, while the one hundred and twenty are not? From this we learn the deeper secret of Sarah, how her particular life influenced everything else that came after her.

The Zohar says:

> "And Sarah's life was..." All this life is above IN BINAH. A hundred year REFERS TO KETER above. "Twenty year" IS CHOCHMAH AND BINAH above. The seven years ARE THE SEVEN LOWER SEFIROT above. THIS IS THE SECRET OF THE FIRST THREE AND THE LOWER SEVEN SEFIROT OF BINAH, WHERE SARAH RECEIVED LIFE, WHICH IS MOCHIN. Rav Shimon said, Come and look at the secret of all this. Why is the number seven followed by the word "years," while all other numbers are followed by the word 'year'? The "hundred year" includes everything, NAMELY KETER, WHICH INCLUDES ALL TEN SEFIROT. EACH

SEFIRAH COMPRISES TEN, AND TOGETHER THEY COMPRISE ONE HUNDRED. For there is included the highest and most secret place of all, WHICH IS ARICH ANPIN, with the hundred daily benedictions, MEANING THAT IT DAILY GIVES THE ABUNDANCE OF A HUNDRED BENEDICTIONS UPON MALCHUT FROM THE HUNDRED SEFIROT IN IT. ARICH ANPIN IS THE SECRET OF KETER OF ATZILUT. Also, the "twenty year," WHICH ARE CHOCHMAH AND BINAH, INCLUDE ARICH ANPIN, the most concealed of all. For that reason, it is written "year" IN THE SINGULAR, which is the secret of unison, for a thought and a Jubilee (Heb. *yovel*). THE SECRET OF CHOCHMAH AND BINAH never separate from each other, AS THE FIRST THREE SEFIROT ARE JOINED TO EACH OTHER AS ONE. But the seven years, WHICH ARE THE SEVEN LOWER SFIROT OF BINAH, are separated from each other and from that which is hidden Above, ARICH ANPIN. Although everything is united and all are equal, THE LOWER SEVEN pertain to Judgment and Mercy in many aspects and paths. This is not so IN THE FIRST THREE SEFIROT OF BINAH, FOR ARICH ANPIN IS ENCLOTHED IN THEM above THE CHEST, WHERE THERE IS NO JUDGEMENT AT ALL. For that reason, it is WRITTEN "SEVEN YEARS" AND NOT "SEVEN year," AS WITH THE FIRST THREE SEFIROT. THE WHOLE TEN SEFIROT, THE FIRST THREE AND LOWER SEVEN, are called life. Therefore it is written, "And Sarah's life was...," for it existed. It was created substantively and existed above, IN THE TEN SEFIROT OF BINAH.

—Zohar, Chayei Sarah 5:23-25

From this section of the Zohar, we see that the portion of Chayei Sarah describes the consciousness that enabled Sarah to conduct a unique life. Through the power of consciousness, Sarah fully controlled her physical state, remaining young in mind and body throughout her life. The number 100 indicates a kabbalistic concept representing 100 different dimensions. These dimensions can appear together in one unified whole—which is our ambition, and what we are to gain from this reading.

The number 100 represents wholeness and unity on the level of Sefira Keter. This number represents the entirety of the Tree of Life according to the elaboration of the ten principal Sefirot, each of which includes within it ten sub-Sefirot (10 x 10=100). Since all the Sefirot are united on the level of Sefira Keter, the Bible has *me'ah shana* (one hundred year), in the singular form rather than the plural. The two Sefirot under Keter—Chochmah and Binah—are represented by the numeral ten, where both have full representation of all the Ten Sefirot, although not to the same degree of completeness as Keter, and therefore they are ten and not 100. The consciousness of unity on the levels of Sefirot Chochmah and Binah is thus defined in the Bible by the words "twenty year," in the singular form and not the plural. The lower Seven Sefirot of the Tree of Life are connected to the material world, and are therefore subject to the illusion of division—which is why *sheva shanim* (seven years) is mentioned in the plural form. Because Sarah succeeded in connecting the Lower Seven Sefirot (Chesed, Gevurah, Tiferet, Netzach, Hod, Yesod, Malchut) with the Upper Three Sefirot (Keter, Chochmah, Binah), she was granted control of mind over matter, mind over the body.

Sarah's Funeral

The Bible says only Abraham came to eulogize and cry for Sarah.
Where was Isaac? Some commentators say Isaac went to the Yeshiva
of Shem and Ever, and thus did not attend Sarah's funeral. This
whole portion is a little strange. The Zohar seems to contradict
what the famous commentator on the Bible, Rashi (Rabbi Shlomo
Yitzchaki, 1040 – 1105) is saying. When Sarah heard that Abraham
was bringing Isaac to be sacrificed, she died. She could not bear
the idea that God would do such a thing, and so she died. We are
discussing Sarah here—the wife of Abraham, who was a chariot and
connected to the Tree of Life, a dimension where there is no death.
In the realm where Abraham and Sarah exist there is no death.
Sarah did not die of a heart attack caused by the shock of hearing
Abraham was preparing to sacrifice Isaac. The Zohar says the Bible
structured it in such a way that first it is written, Sarah lived a
hundred and twenty seven years, and then she died. The Zohar
explains that she had completed the full circle of all of the Ten
Sefirot, and that once she had completed all she was destined to do
in this physical world, she then realized why Abraham took Isaac to
be slaughtered. Did Sarah really believe Abraham was going to kill
him? No, Sarah understood the purpose of the Binding of Isaac. It
was to bring together the Right and the Left Columns—Abraham
and Isaac. Isaac was not tempered. Isaac was Desire to Receive, and
there was no Central Column as yet because Jacob had not been
born. The Binding of Isaac created a Desire to Receive for the Sake
of Sharing within Isaac. When Sarah heard this had been achieved,
she knew the stage was now set for Jacob to enter the scene. Sarah
did not die; she realized that her manifestation in this world
had come to an end. She had completed the whole circle, just as
Abraham had completed the circle—now they were ready for the
new stage.

Appreciation of Life and Resurrection of the Dead

Chayei Sarah, which means "Life of Sarah," deals with only one thing: life. The emphasis in this portion is on ways to connect with life, ways to strengthen the force of life, and ways to enliven things and people who have died—or allegedly died. This creates an opening for a huge change within because it enables us to succeed in areas or with the things we have given up on until now. At one time the invention of the wheel was considered a miracle, and the idea of humans landing on the moon was considered imaginary, unrealistic. So too, is the concept of the revival or Resurrection of the Dead now considered impossible. Yet the Resurrection of the Dead is as practical and as possible as landing on the moon. And the day when we will observe its fulfillment is much closer than most of us think. There is a vicious circle here because a precondition for the actualization of the Resurrection of the Dead is achieving a critical mass of people who believe it is probable and possible. Whoever is undecided, and waits to be shown a miracle before joining the circle of believers, slows down the process, thus preventing it from occurring. This is the disadvantage of our physical material approach to the matter: "I am a simple man from the state of Missouri, show me, and then I'll believe..." We have to believe it is possible first and then, depending on our merit, it will occur before our very eyes.

There are many people who do not live life but merely exist in it and for this reason they cannot reach a state of true appreciation. When someone just exists—they do not see what they really have—they only subsist on the most basic level. All too often, people are only able to truly appreciate after they experience a loss, and this is not real appreciation. Realizing the truth only after loss is simply a response or a reaction to an existing situation. Real appreciation is gratitude for all the moments in life. Sarah lived 127 years, meaning she appreciated each and every minute of her existence in this physical dimension. The way to stay in true appreciation is to understand that, in an instant, everything can be lost.

Kiriath Arba and the Tetragrammaton

In the second verse it is written that "Sarah died in Kiriath Arba, that is Hebron." She did not die of old age but parted peacefully from the physical body which had served her up to that day. Sarah was completely in touch with the Tree of Life, and for this reason her body was buried in a sacred place. The word *arba* is Hebrew for the number four. It is also a reference to the Tetragrammaton—ה.ו.ה.י—the four letters of the Holy Name of God, which is the means of communicating with the Tree of Life and the Force that enables the Resurrection of the Dead. Scripture adds the phrase "that is Hebron" to teach us that the Tetragrammaton connected Sarah to eternal life—and it can also connect us. The Hebrew word Hebron (חברון) is from the same root as *lechaber* (לחבר), which means "to join together." The message of this portion is not only about the worldly life of Sarah coming to a close. The story reminds us Sarah lived all the days of her life in wholeness and unity with the universe—in the consciousness of *Mashiach* (Messiah). Sarah appreciated every moment in her life, and this is why she was granted control over it. We tend to take every routine aspect of our lives for granted, and we only remember to appreciate it as a reaction to losing it. Appreciating life and health only when visiting a hospital or a graveyard is not genuine appreciation. Such appreciation passes quickly. The portion of Chayei Sarah, which means "Life of Sarah," connects us to the consciousness of Sarah, who managed to truly appreciate life and was thus constantly connected to it.

The Kabbalah Centre and the Small Letter Kaf

In the Kabbalah Centres we provide information about life; information that can affect, influence, and contribute to the entire cosmic process. What is the purpose of the Kabbalah Centres? Is it to teach the wisdom of Rav Ashlag or Rav Brandwein? And what were the intentions of these two men? Was it to give out information? Has information ever changed the world? Look at Newton, at Einstein. Have they changed the nature of humanity, have they affected the natural order of things? The world behaves according to its ways, according to suffering and problems. What therefore is the goal of the Kabbalah Centres?

I would like to mention here that Rav Avraham Azulai (1570 - 1643), says the time in which we are living now is a time for great change—a time for the transformation of nature, a time for miracles and wonders. Rav Ashlag and Rav Brandwein have given us the knowledge of transformation. Without the knowledge of Kabbalah, life is filled with danger and death. I have only recently understood that learning this wisdom and applying the technology is physical life itself.

The way to transform the information we receive from the study of Kabbalah into knowledge is by means of the power of resistance or restriction. And the way to bring about restriction is to influence rather than be influenced—to be the cause not the effect. The small letter *Kaf* hints at Malchut, which is Isaac's companion. It is also the result of the action of influencing rather than being influenced. Trading stocks and bonds is really a basic reaction to present conditions, values rising or falling. There is no invention or creation taking place in this trading. A person who is considered to be a genius at buying and selling stocks is, in reality, merely continuously reacting to situations as they unfold at the stock exchange; he does not himself initiate any action.

The force of one who influences, creates new conditions. If a sick man, being influenced by his present condition, wants to become a philanthropist, wants to give to charity, and even prays to the Creator, he is not summoning up a new situation. This sick man may be performing positive acts but, unfortunately, his actions are simply a reaction to his present condition of illness, rather than arising from any new condition he has created himself.

Similarly, if I see a cake and very much wish to have it, what is actually happening? The cake looks at me and tells me I have to eat it now. If I take the cake in accordance with what the cake wants from me, then I am being influenced by the cake. I may think that declining the cake for a moment is enough—I made a show of resistance, so now I can eat it with a clear conscience. But in doing this I am not a creator of influence, because I am still being influenced. The purpose of Kabbalah is to teach us how to create a new situation; one in which we understand that we really do not need the cake and do not actually even want it. Now we can take the cake with a different kind of awareness—we are the cause not the effect. Many people think that a kabbalist does not have great desires but, in fact, a kabbalist has very great desires—except a kabbalist knows the difference between being the creator of a situation or the result of a situation.

Satan's great weapon is the doubt he continually attempts to instill in us, the doubt that affects every area of our lives. Satan can penetrate even spiritual places. To annihilate all doubts and the entirety of Satan, we must connect to the power of being a creator of influence, and not be a slave to our present conditions.

Small Kaf, Large Letters and Binah

What is the meaning of the little *Kaf*? There are three sizes of letters used in the Torah Scroll—large, regular, and small. For example, the large letter *Bet* in the word Beresheet (the first portion in the Book of Beresheet) helps us enter into the inner consciousness of the Sefira of Binah. Binah is the very source, the actual storehouse of all Light. On Yom Kippur, the cosmos opens the Gates of Enlightenment and takes us into the dimension of Binah. If we believe that on Yom Kippur God forgives us, we are in fact misunderstanding the meaning and the opportunity available to us. What about the rest of the year? For the last 2,000 years, since the time of Rav Shimon, we have forgotten this truth. After his death, we reverted to a dark age of ignorance. On Yom Kippur, we attain forgiveness by entering into Binah and tapping into the enormous Light there—and then the darkness simply fades away.

This is the second time in the Bible that there is a significant small letter. The first time a small letter appears is in the second chapter of Beresheet—the letter *Hei*—which is the connection to the physical world. The objective in the *tikkun* process (spiritual correction) is to reduce the physical reality for as long as it remains with us. What has recently become conventional wisdom is that what is more is less, and what is less is more. A table made from wood appears to be solid yet science tells us the table is, in fact, ninety-nine percent space and not physical matter. Science has changed the thinking about the nature of physical reality but we also need to reduce its influence in our consciousness, and reduce it to the point where we can accept the possibility of walking through a wall. The 1 Percent Reality, our material world, is the domain of Satan, the realm where both good and evil exist, side by side. It is because evil exists that we cannot fly. Physical reality is a minute portion of the true reality—and we ought to be able to walk through a wall.

It is written in the Bible, "And Sarah died at Kiriath Arba, that is Hebron in the land of Canaan, and Abraham went in to mourn for Sarah and to weep for her." Why is it that people cry when a body is placed in the ground? It is because they are sure that they will no longer see the person who was close to them. When the coffin is covered with earth and the deceased is no longer visible, this is often the moment of the greatest grief because we base so much of our perception on physical sight.

In the book *Chesed leAvraham*, Rav Avraham Azulai explains that during the days of the *Mashiach* (Messiah), those not connected to the Light will live as though they are suffering an extreme electric shock. What Abraham Azulai says is that during this period of the Resurrection of the Dead, people will not be able to handle the transformation of reality from nature to miracle. They will not be able to withstand the change from thousands of years of suffering, death, and disease to a state of renewal—a state where, for example, someone who loses an arm will grow the limb back. Abraham Azulai says that those who are not ready for this may well die. The Zohar's commentary on the portion of Shemot also states that there will be those who will want to kill the *Mashiach* because they will not be able to withstand the transformation from nature to miracle. Therefore, the purpose of the Kabbalah Centres is to prepare our awareness so that we are not in a state of shock when there is a change from nature to miracle. We can only understand this through meditation and prayer.

Rav Isaac Luria (the Ari, 1534 – 1572) and the Zohar explain how the small letter *Kaf* helps us control the world of nature and it tells us that Sarah did not die—just as Moses, Rav Shimon, and Joseph did not die. In *Sefer haLikutim*, the Ari explains that following a person's death, the mourning period should be seven days and no longer—three days, and no more, are allocated for crying, and four days for eulogies and remembrance of the good deeds done by the person who left this world. Crying is therefore valued less than the eulogies. Crying is connected with nature, with this world, with the world of illusion. Eulogies are connected with the soul, with the Upper World, which is why there are more days allocated to it.

The Zohar says that when Rav Shimon left this world, his son Rav Elazar cried. Yet his tears were not for his own loss but rather he cried for the world that would no longer benefit from his father's level of consciousness, from Rav Shimon's light.

Why is crying limited to three days and the rest allocated for eulogizing? It is because Sarah did not die. What happened, as we understand it, is that her physical body ceased to exist relative to the observer. When the coffin is covered, the tears flow. Why? At that moment the deceased is gone from our sight. Before that moment, while the coffin is still visible, we somehow experience our loved ones among us, still among the living. Once the coffin is buried, we no longer see the deceased and we feel that the deceased no longer sees us. We feel we have lost sight of one another. Moses did not die. Yet when he was gone the Israelites assumed he was dead. We feel the same way at times when our loved ones are no longer in our physical presence.

If we can elevate our consciousness, we can achieve immortality and regenerate ourselves. We should be getting younger; we should be reversing the aging process, for it is in our power to do so. The aging process is in our consciousness, and once we change our thought process we will experience the reversal of aging.

After a death, if instead of crying for more than three days about our loss, we remember the good deeds of the person who has passed, we can begin to feel their presence with us, and so they become alive again. Taken one step further, this *Kaf* shows us how to begin to reduce and then eliminate the aging process. We have to raise our consciousness. We are constantly fighting the physical reality of death when we really should be focusing on overcoming it with our consciousness. We are so caught up in only recognizing physicality to the point that we forget God is not only available to us once a year but the Light of the Creator is here every day.

Reducing Ego, Difficulties and Lack

In the second verse we find the small letter *Kaf* [כ] in the word *velivkota* (to weep for her). A small letter in the Torah scroll denotes the Sefira of Malchut. What is the meaning of the small *Kaf*? What is the connection with Malchut? With the section of Chayei Sarah we come to recognize the power of small things. Everything is getting smaller, and technology is an obvious example of this. The small *Kaf* stimulates the physical reality to grow smaller until it is reduced to nothing. The idea of the power of consciousness over matter is demonstrated at the end of the verse through the reduced letter *Kaf*. The numerical value of *Kaf* is 20, which is equal to Ten Sefirot of Direct Light plus Ten Sefirot of Reflected Light. Malchut is the tenth Sefira and its role is to reveal, through the power of resistance (by means of Returning or Reflected Light), the Direct Light that is poured into it through all the other Sefirot. The letter *Kaf* represents the world of illusion, the world of matter in which people experience difficulties, feel lack and sorrow. By reducing the letter we reduce the emotions that are connected with illusion such as doubt, confusion, poverty, frustration, sorrow, and suffering, while we strengthen the consciousness of the world of truth, joy, certainty, and freedom from chaos. This is the power of consciousness over matter.

The Three Kafs of Humanity

Rav Abraham Azulai says that, for most of us, our ego establishes
how we treat people. Our perception is that someone who is
wealthy is smart, while a beggar must be the opposite. This, of
course, is not always true. This is how society currently evaluates
intelligence, though, because everything is tied to the ego.

The letter *Kaf* is a very noteworthy letter for a kabbalist. The three
Kafs that bring us down are *kavod* (our honor and standing in life),
kiseh (our chair or our position, title), and *ka'as* (anger). The reason
not to be full of ego is because it does not pay, not because we are
unimportant. It will bring us down. At the Kabbalah Centres, we
have thrown the notion of morals and ethics out the window. We
do not discuss how we are "supposed" to behave for the sake of
morality. Someone recently said that at the Kabbalah Centres we are
politically incorrect; we do not conform the way all other religious
institutions do. I liked this comment because religion is politics,
and we are politically incorrect. We do not conform to politics and
we never will, because you should not mix politics with spirituality.
Are we to understand from the portion of Lech Lecha that it was
a just act for Abraham to slaughter his son? Or from the Book of
Bemidbar, was it right that every man, woman, and child that was
not an Israelite should be killed? We have gone along with this way
of thinking for 3,400 years.

Rav Azulai and the Zohar both say the reason we do not kill, steal
or commit many other offenses is not because it is politically
or morally incorrect but rather because it simply does not pay.
The reason not to steal, not to kill, and the reason to pay our
taxes is because it pays to do so. It will provide us with serenity,
contentment, and all the luxury in the world. This is why we
refrain from negativity and engage in positivity—and not because
it is morally correct. The small *Kaf* assists our consciousness to rise

above the need for *kavod* (the honor or ego) and everything else we strive for that is an impediment to our efforts to receive that which will enhance our lives.

3 And Abraham rose from beside his dead, and spoke to the sons of Heth, saying, 4 "I am an alien and a stranger among you; give me possession of a burial site here so I may bury my dead out of sight." 5 And the children of Heth answered Abraham, saying to him, 6 "Hear us, my lord, you are a mighty prince among us; bury your dead in the choicest of our tombs. None of us will refuse you his tomb for burying your dead." 7 And Abraham rose and bowed himself down before the people of the land, to the children of Heth. 8 And he communed with them, saying, "If you are willing to let me bury my dead out of sight, hear me and intercede with Ephron, son of Zohar, on my behalf, 9 so he will give me the Cave of Machpelah, which belongs to him and is at the end of his field, for the full price as a burial site among you." 10 And Ephron dwelt among the children of Heth, and Ephron the Hittite answered Abraham in the presence of all the Hittites who had come to the gate of his city, saying, 11 "No, my lord, hear me; I give you the field, and I give you the cave that is in it. I give it to you in the presence of my people. Bury your dead." 12 And Abraham bowed himself down before the people of the land. 13 And he said to Ephron in the presence of the people of the land, saying, "But if you will give it, I pray you hear me, I will give you money for the field. Accept it from me so I can bury my dead there." 14 And Ephron answered Abraham, saying, 15 "Listen to me, my lord; the land is worth

four hundred shekels of silver, but what is that between me and you? Bury your dead."

Burial Site for Sarah

In this section of the Bible, there is a full description of Abraham's efforts to acquire the gravesite for his wife, where subsequently Isaac and Rebecca, and Jacob and Leah would also be buried. According to the Zohar, this was the place where Adam and Eve were buried. The cave was not obvious to anyone except Abraham, who once followed a stray calf into this cave, where he actually saw Adam.

The Business Proposition

Although this land was promised to the Israelites, Abraham entered into negotiations to buy the burial ground, teaching us how we should conduct ourselves in business, as well as what it means to follow the universal principles. Abraham knew which cave he wanted but he did not want to let Ephron know which one it was. Abraham restricted, teaching us that in business it is beneficial to use restriction. Business is not to be separated from our spirituality. The Bible talks about universal principles, and we know that, in not following these spiritual laws of the universe, we will fall into chaos. Murphy's Law about what can go wrong only exists on this level. Through the Bible, we learn to connect with the universal laws that govern this world, rather than religion.

Abraham conducted this transaction by applying the power of resistance and in maintaining his certainty in the Light. He did not show eagerness and was not ready to pay any price. His certainty in the Light may have been expressed in this way: "If I am worthy, this cave will be mine, and this transaction will also succeed at a price that will be an amazing bargain. Whereas if I am not worthy of it, even if I would purchase it for a very high price, I would not have the privilege of using it and it would in some way be taken away from me." The process of negotiation was three-sided rather than two-sided, which is another way to reveal the energy of the Central Column, the balancing aspect of the Three Column System, through which the Light is revealed.

Energy Centres in the World

This cave is a very significant place and its energy is what we want to receive from this portion of the Bible. Places have significance. For example, the site where the Holy Temple is located in Jerusalem is highly significant. There are certain energy centers all around the world. The cave is not holy because Abraham, Isaac, and Jacob are buried there. This cave was, in and of itself, a place that had powerful energy. When Abraham first came to the cave, he discovered that this place radiates the infinite Lightforce of God. The fact that Abraham chose to have Sarah buried there is another indication that physical people like these can act as channels to help us to reach into this awesome Light.

The verses, stories, and numbers found in the Bible can seem meaningless, but these Hebrew letters, words, and phrases are our way of making connections to an immaterial, non-physical energy-force that we otherwise have no access to at all. Therefore, we have these people—Adam and Eve, Abraham, Sarah, Isaac, Rebecca, Jacob and Leah—who are in this particular place, to help us obtain access. The point here is that specific people, not only Joseph or Rav Shimon, have come to this world to provide us with a way to access the Lightforce of God.

Energy Sites and Burial Places

There is a beautiful picture showing a ray of the sun shining down on the grave of the High Priest Yehoyada, which is situated deep in a canyon in Safed, Israel. Climbing down the steep hill to reach this grave can put one's life in jeopardy. Why would a High Priest, living in Jerusalem, want to be buried in such a remote place? There are seventy-six energy centers in this world that exist to help us to tap into the Lightforce of God. These locations reflect a little more Light to the world. Many of them are places where people are buried. The Zohar explains that when Rav Shimon passed away, there was a disagreement between the people as to where he should be buried. Each person wanted him to be buried in their town, so they could pray near to a *tzadik* (a righteous person). The Zohar says that Rav Shimon's bed lifted into the air and carried his body to the place where Rav Shimon himself wanted his body to be buried. The same is true in the story of Sarah; no one carried her to the cave. These ancient people were so elevated they could recognize if a place was an energy source.

Many people think that Jerusalem is a holy city because the Holy Temple is located there. Rav Shimon says no physical experience can ever provide us with a cause or reason for an event. The fact that the Temple is there is not the cause. How can these energy centers be recognized? Jerusalem is one, and Hebron is another. Great souls have made their home there, so when we are in need of more Light, we know where to go as God's presence is there. When we go to these energy centers this is what we are looking for. The righteous souls were tested so that we could find the Light that we need so badly in our lives.

Through the letters, words, and verses of this biblical portion we can tap into the energy of this place. This is what this portion concerns.

It is the formulation of these letters and verses that will permit us to tap into this awesome energy.

For the past 2,000 years, Jewish people have prayed three times a day, and these three prayers correspond to Abraham, Isaac, and Jacob. There is something that stands above the power of Abraham, Isaac, and Jacob, and that is the power of the place where they are buried. It is not a coincidence that they are buried in Hebron. Because in Hebron there is the possibility of connecting to the world's library of metaphysical knowledge, where it is possible to unite with the wisdom of the past and connect with the knowledge of tomorrow. This is one of the reasons Sarah is buried there.

16 And Abraham agreed to Ephron's terms and weighed out for him the price he had named in the presence of the Hittites: four hundred shekels of silver, current with the merchant. 17 And the field of Ephron in Machpelah, which was before Mamre—both the field and the cave in it, and all the trees that were in the field, that were within the borders of the field—were deeded 18 to Abraham as his property in the presence of all the Hittites who had come to the gate of his city.

Four Hundred Worlds of Pleasure

Abraham weighed the money and gave it to Ephron. What did he give him and why was Ephron satisfied with this money? The Zohar says that when Abraham gave Ephron the money, it contained the pleasure of the four hundred worlds. There are four hundred different aspects of pleasure in the world. We all derive pleasure: some through food; others through accomplishments in business; some in seeing a beautiful person; others in gaining knowledge. When Abraham gave the 400 shekels, Ephron was satisfied because as he took the money, he felt he was gaining every pleasure possible in exchange for what he was giving. After a buy-sell deal is concluded, both parties cry. The seller cries because he thinks he sold it too cheap. The buyer cries because he thinks he paid too much. Why is this the case? It is because neither of them feels pleasure. They feel robbed in some way. They feel that something is missing—pleasure. When we buy a business, a house, an apartment, or even when we buy clothing, it is common to bargain for the best possible deal. The problem with negotiating is that each is trying to get the maximum out of the deal at the expense of the other person. What one gets, the other does not. Pleasure is not included, therefore things can go wrong. Abraham behaved in such a way that Ephron should never regret having sold his piece of land. Abraham knew what this piece of property was and how to connect with it. He also understood that it really belonged to him. The Zohar elaborates further that Ephron was so happy he had rid himself of this land because it did not belong to him.

It is like owning a building that not only eats its own profit, it also drains the other businesses in order to keep it fed. Why does one get into business? Why do we work so hard? It is because we want to have some of the good things in life. A miser may just want to accumulate money, but most people want money so they can have the better things in life—at least the things that money can buy, such as a better suit, the ability to travel, a better home. Most people do not want money as an end in itself but rather as a means. Yet we are still not satisfied—and this is because we do not know how to connect to the source.

The reason the Bible calls this place Kiriath Arba is because this is where the Tetragrammaton—*Yud, Hei, Vav*, and *Hei*—originates. It is the spiritual entrance to the Garden of Eden, to the Tree of Life. It is the main frame of everything, which is why the *four* couples are buried there—Adam and Eve, Abraham and Sarah, Isaac and Rebecca, Jacob and Leah. Each couple represents a quarter of the selling price—a hundred shekels—because all four make the connection. When we want to make a connection through prayer, especially in the Amida, we want to be with Abraham, Isaac, and Jacob because without a connection to them we do not make a connection at all. We do not gain access to the necessary information. This is the purpose for which these four couples are buried in this location.

Come and behold, if Ephron had seen in the cave what Abraham saw, he would never have sold it. But because Ephron saw nothing in it, as nothing is revealed except to its owner, it was revealed to Abraham only and not to Ephron. It was revealed to Abraham because it was his, and not Ephron's, for Ephron had no share in it. Therefore Ephron saw nothing of the cave. He saw only darkness and therefore, he sold it.

Moreover, he also sold him what Abraham did not ask him to sell, because Abraham said only, "That he may give me the Cave of the Machpelah... for the full price he shall give it me" (Beresheet 23:8) and did not mention the field. And Ephron said, "The field I give you, and the cave that is in it, I give it you," (Ibid. 11) for Ephron knew not what it was and found it all loathsome. Even the field, in which the cave was, was loathsome to him. Therefore he sold the field too, although Abraham did not ask for it.
—Zohar, Chayei Sarah 16:103-104

The Zohar says that when Abraham came to buy this place, the Cave of Machpelah, he did not point to the location he wanted, although he did know exactly what he wanted. Instead he came to the people of Heth and said he would like to bury his wife, and then allowed them to choose the place. He was also of a mind that he would pay whatever they asked of him. Ephron, the owner of the land known as Cave of Machpelah, came forward. The Zohar explains that we are meant to learn from Abraham's behavior. Although Abraham had a desire for this specific piece of land, he did not speak to Ephron directly but rather he spoke to the whole tribe of Heth. The Zohar says that what we are meant to learn from this transaction is that if we have a desire for something, we are not meant to approach directly. Instead we leave room for that which is truly ours to come to us—that which is not ours will ultimately never come to us. The Zohar prefaces this by saying that Abraham knew this place belonged to him because when he made the connection, the Garden of Eden opened up to him. Just because he wanted it would not have been a sufficient reason for him to say, "Give it to me."

If we are connected to the Light—and it takes a lot of time to want to be on that frequency—that which belongs to us will come to us, and the person who has what is ours will want to get rid of it because it does not belong to them. The Zohar says this is what we are supposed to be learning from the transaction.

19 And after this Abraham buried his wife Sarah in the cave in the field of Machpelah before Mamre, which is at Hebron in the land of Canaan. 20 And the field and the cave in it were deeded to Abraham by the sons of Heth as a burial site.

Eve and Sarah in the Cave

People who have experienced clinical death often describe a similar occurrence: Coming to a cave or tunnel, and at the end there is a light. They very much want to run towards this light, to become attached to it. But then a voice will say, "No, not yet," and then they recede from the light and come back into their bodies. The Zohar explains that this light is the form of Adam in the Cave of Machpelah in Hebron. When Abraham entered the cave on a previous occasion, he saw the form of Adam and he knew then that this was the place to bury Sarah.

The Zohar, in Chayei Sarah 16:105, says:

> Come and behold, when Abraham entered the cave for the first time, he saw a light. The dust was removed from before him, revealing two graves. Adam rose from his grave in his rightful form, saw Abraham, and laughed. By that, Abraham knew that he was destined to be buried there.

And continues:

> Rabbi Shimon said, "When Abraham entered the cave and brought Sarah thither, Adam and Eve rose and did not want Sarah to be buried there. They said, 'It is it not enough for us that we are in disgrace in the world before the Holy One,

blessed be He, because of the sin that we committed, but now we will further be put to shame because of your good deeds.'"

—Zohar, Chayei Sarah 16:108

Here, the Zohar teaches us something interesting in the form of an unusual discussion that took place between Sarah and Eve. When Abraham brought Sarah into this place to be buried, Eve, the wife of Adam who was also buried there, saw Sarah arriving so she left. Eve said, "I cannot bear to be here in the same place as Sarah. Because I convinced Adam to eat from the Tree of Knowledge, the world continues on with suffering. And as Sarah was such a righteous woman, I would feel embarrassment to have her next to me in this cave." The embarrassment was so great that Eve walked out. The Zohar continues, explaining that, as Eve walked out, Sarah said, "I will pray for you, and my prayers will alleviate any reminder of my righteousness and any disturbance my presence will cause you." Hearing these words, Eve returned to the cave, content now to be buried there.

The Meaning of 400 Shekels

Why is it so important to know exactly how much Abraham paid Ephron for the cave and land? Why did Abraham not approach Ephron directly but instead conducted the whole negotiation in front of "the people of the land"? It is because the connection to the World of Truth became stronger when the Machpelah Cave was purchased. The matter of the Machpelah Cave and its purchase is explained at length in the Zohar, Chayei Sarah 88-93.

The Zohar makes the point that this story is not to be considered literal in any way—not that the story is not factual. The purpose of the Bible, however, is not to record the purchase of this significant piece of property. Certainly, had the significance of the land been known, it would not have been sold for a mere 400 shekels. If someone has a known interest to buy a piece of real estate, the price goes up. The reason is simple: desire knows no bounds.

As time goes on, we unravel more mysteries and more codes surrounding each story of the Bible. The stories are encrypted so that the layers of secrets will be revealed. The idea of 400 shekels paid for the gravesite was not just a number that was arrived at randomly. The Ari wrote a whole section about the 400 pieces of silver. Moreover, this is not the only reference to the number 400. When Esau arrived with the intention to "eliminate" Jacob, he approached with 400 people. What is the relevance of stating this number? Is it possible that there were exactly 400 and not 399 or 401? The number 400 is a communication with eternal life since it removes all possible impurities. The 400 shekels correspond to the 400 Gates of Impurity contained in the material world. When a person immerses in a *mikveh* (ritual bath for spiritual cleansing), the volume of water is at least 40 *se'a* (a form of measurement), and each *se'a* removes ten degrees of negativity. Therefore connecting to the reading of Chayei Sarah is like a non-physical immersion in a *mikveh* with the power to clean chaos, the power of eternal life, and the Resurrection of the Dead.

Mamre, Hebron and Klipot

There is an additional connection to eternal life and the Resurrection of the Dead through the word Mamre—a physical location—mentioned twice in this portion. The word *mamre* [ממרא] has the same numerical value as the five final letters of the Hebrew alphabet: *Mem, Nun, Tzadik, Pei, Chaf* [ם.ן.ץ.ף.ך]. These letters represent a connection to and an activation of the Resurrection of the Dead. In Beresheet 23:17-19, when Abraham purchased the Machpelah Cave from Ephron, he connected to the positive aspect of the place and isolated it from the negative aspects surrounding it.

Hebron is a significant point of energy, and because of the Light found there, certain *klipot* (negative shells) attach themselves so as to be nourished by the Light. In biblical times, Hebron was one of the six shelter towns. People with blood on their hands would dwell there. Hebron is also the "flaming sword which turned every way" (Beresheet 3:24) at the gate of the Garden of Eden. On one hand there is a connection to the Light, and on the other it is a sword that can bring destruction.

The name Ephron comes from the same root as the Hebrew word *afar*, which means "dust." This represents the hold that the *klipot* have on the field of Machpelah, the very heart of Hebron, and the gate to the Garden of Eden and the World of Truth. By this purchase, Abraham redeemed the field of Machpelah from the *klipot*, and thereby opened for humanity a clean and powerful connection to a central communication channel to the Light of Ein Sof, the Endless Light.

Beresheet 24:1 And Abraham was old and well advanced in age, and the Lord had blessed Abraham in every way.

A Full Life and the Power of the Soulmate

In Hebrew, the expression *ba bayamim* refers to one who is advanced in age; however, it literally means "came in the days." The text says *ba bayamim* in relation to Abraham, telling us that every day of Abraham's life was full. A person may live 70 years in one day or live one day in 70 years. It depends on the fullness of their life.

There is always a connection between the weekly Bible portion and the Haftarah read in conjunction with it that week. The Haftarah of Chayei Sarah (1 Melachim 1:1-13) states, "Now King David was old and advanced in years." The same expression that is used in relation to Abraham, *ba bayamim*, is also used for King David because King David's days were also full. In this Haftarah it is unclear who will rule after David. The prophet Nathan spoke to Batsheva and told her to go to the king and remind him he had taken an oath that Solomon would rule after him. Concerning Abraham, there was no question who would continue after him because after Sefira Chesed comes Sefira Gevurah, which is Isaac. But King David is Sefira Malchut, therefore it was not clear who would be king after him. Batsheva was David's true soulmate, and as Solomon was the son of Batsheva and David, he would rule after King David.

This Haftarah tells us that there was a single consideration for choosing Solomon as David's successor—the blessing and the continuity of cosmic partnership. When there is a bond between partners, there is continuity and communication with the root. Business partners are of secondary importance, because the soulmate makes a bond with the source, and from this portion one can receive the power of the soulmate.

2 And Abraham said to the chief servant in his household, the one in charge of all that he had, "Put, I pray you, your hand under my thigh. 3 And I will make you swear by the Lord, the God of Heaven and the God of Earth, that you will not take a wife for my son from the daughters of the Canaanites, among whom I am living. 4 But you will go to my country and my own kind and take a wife for my son Isaac." 5 And the servant asked him, "What if the woman is unwilling to come back with me to this land? Shall I then take your son back to the land from which you came?" 6 And Abraham said, "Beware that you do not take my son back there again. 7 The Lord God of Heaven, Who brought me out of my father's house and from the land of my kind and Who spoke to me and promised me on oath, saying, 'To your seed I will give this land,' He will send His angel before you so that you can get a wife for my son from there. 8 And if the woman is unwilling to come back with you, then you will be released from this oath of mine. Only do not take my son back there." 9 And the servant put his hand under the thigh of Abraham, his master, and swore an oath to him concerning this matter.

Eliezer's Oath

Why did Abraham instruct his chief servant Eliezer to take a vow that he would not bring back a daughter-in-law not of his liking? If he did bring back a girl from a nation or a family that Abraham did not favor, could Abraham not say, "This girl is not for my son Isaac"? Why did he insist on Eliezer taking a vow? I will answer these questions in several parts.

Let us first examine what is a vow. The Zohar says the word *neder* means "a promise," and the word *shevu'ah* is a "vow or oath." But what do both promise and oath represent? It is consciousness. The Zohar explains that this is the true reality of life. The action of stealing or murdering is secondary to the consciousness of stealing or murdering. After all, why does someone kill or steal? It is consciousness. The reason a person pays for his crime is not because of the action—the action represents only one percent of reality—but because of his consciousness. What is presented in the Bible through the study of Kabbalah is that there is nothing in this world but consciousness.

The Zohar explains that a thief pays the price for stealing because of the reality of his consciousness, which dictates to his mind the fact that he has decided to steal. If he does not steal, then there is no materialization of this consciousness. However, what is significant is the consciousness. The Bible is teaching us that, where our consciousness is, is also where we are. If we are a thief in our consciousness, getting caught is secondary.

In the Kol Nidrei connection on Yom Kippur, we cancel or nullify our vows. Kol Nidrei is the most important part of the Yom Kippur cosmic event. Yom Kippur is traditionally considered the time when we ask God to forgive us for cheating and stealing, and for all the wrong things we have done; it is a time of repentance. Yet Kol Nidrei does not discuss repentance—in the Kol Nidrei we do not ask for forgiveness. It is natural to assume that we would be asking God for forgiveness in the most important part of the connection. Why is the nullification of vows the most important feature? When we say Kol Nidrei, we nullify and cancel those vows that we did not fulfill. The Zohar explains that the moment we say, "I promise" or "I will do," the action has already been done. This is the way the natural laws and principles of the universe operate. The minute we say, "I am giving," we are immediately rewarded because we have accomplished ninety-nine percent of the action. If we promise to give a dollar to charity today, that charity receives a dollar. However, there is a requirement of the one percent action to give the physical dollar. On the other hand, if we promise and we do not fulfill that one percent, then we have received this reward without having fulfilled the one percent requirement, which means we have received something for nothing—we received the energy but did not follow through. This is often the way life works.

Kol Nidrei is the most important part of Yom Kippur because it deals with consciousness and not whether we cheated or stole. After all, on the physical level we can return what is stolen. But what about a negative action that we have thrust into the cosmos? When good people suddenly act in intolerant or negative ways, it is because the cosmos is so filled with negative consciousness. This is the problem today. Kol Nidrei is to remove the negative consciousness and not the negative actions. When we think with evil or intolerance, we have already impregnated the cosmos with this negativity.

Kabbalah explains there is nothing but consciousness—where our head is at is where we are at. When we understand the importance of consciousness, we raise our own consciousness. And with that we come to understand what the Dark Lord does not permit the majority of people in the world to understand—that we should be happy, thank God for every moment that we breathe, and for the ability to eat food because in one moment it can be gone, God forbid.

One moment someone may be on a balcony overlooking the ocean enjoying a party, and the next moment that balcony collapses. The Zohar says that having security in tomorrow comes with the understanding of how insecure things are now. When we consciously inject insecurity into our consciousness, then we are asking of God—no, we are demanding of God!—that God will be with us every minute of every day. But along comes the Dark Lord, injecting the notion into our thoughts: "Things are good. Why are you asking God to be with you, the business is great, you have a wonderful family relationship, why do you need God now?"

Security is not something you can buy. It may be called life insurance but when is it collected? Upon your death. We fall into these traps, yet according to the Zohar, there is a period when we can access life insurance, and it is known as Shavuot. We cannot pay money for it but we can have it. The Dark Lord's function is to lure us into a false sense of security. He keeps us from understanding that we have no permanent security. We do not have it—not even if we achieve the consciousness of appreciating God for giving us every breath, knowing that in a moment it can all disappear. We can still come back to God when things do not go so great and say, "God where are you? I have had 50 great years and now suddenly they are not so great..." We need to remember what the Zohar tells us that if we want God, He is here. We all want and need to be wired with God in our consciousness—and nothing more.

Does this mean we can do nothing all day, and God will be with us simply because we think God is with us? No, there is the one percent physical reality to deal with. We have to be part of this reality. To check in regularly to see that, even when we have a problem, we are still appreciating God for every minute we are alive. If we appreciate and need God every second, God will never disappear.

Is our consciousness thanking God that the business is going well or do we only call upon God after the business has taken a turn for the worse and the accountant cannot help? If the latter is the case, then, at that moment, we lose touch with being wired into the Lightforce of God.

We are wired into God when we understand that everything we have comes from the Lightforce of God. It should not be that when things are good it is thanks to me and when suddenly things go bad, we ask where God is. The Dark Lord has been given permission to provide us with each problem—but only to strengthen our connection with the Lightforce. This is why we at the Kabbalah Centres call problems opportunities. This way of seeing things requires consciousness and it is what Abraham was telling Eliezer. Abraham asked Eliezer to swear an oath because he knew that if Eliezer made him a promise, Eliezer would not be guided by his robotic consciousness. The physical human body, if compressed, is one percent of the space we occupy. Everything that we have, every thought that comes to us, is not ours. Are we conscious when we talk? Think about it. We have no choice, we are robotic. The question is one of, "Are we wired into the Lightforce?" When wired to the Lightforce, we do not make mistakes; whereas when we are not, the Dark Lord makes sure we speak stupidly. Consciousness is all that we possess.

All the precepts that we were given on Mount Sinai were to keep the Dark Lord at bay—nothing more, nothing less. It has nothing to do with the Lightforce. It has nothing to do with being in the service of the Lord. It has nothing to do with "doing it so God will give me goody points after 120 years." In advising us not steal, it is so we should be aware of not putting negativity into the cosmos, not because we should be "good." The Talmud says that a small measure of intolerance for one's neighbor was reason enough for the destruction of the Temple. Hatred for no reason means I cannot bear it that someone has what I have. It is irrational.

We need to achieve the awareness that there is more than enough abundance in the world for everyone and that the world was created to be in balance. Should there be rich and poor? Yes, because these two conditions provide the aspects of sharing and receiving, which create balance in the entire universe. The world is balanced. Humankind, with our inhumanity, with evil consciousness, creates the chaos. This is what the Zohar wants to teach us: raise our consciousness, not to become a better person but so that we can have everything that was originally intended for us to receive. God's Thought of Creation was to provide for everyone; it was not His idea to play Holocaust games with us.

Power of Swearing an Oath

Why did Abraham make his servant Eliezer make a vow if later in the text Abraham tells Eliezer that, if the woman he finds does not want to return with him, he must let her go? Why was the oath necessary? Abraham had the ability to control reality through the World of Truth, which is the 99 Percent Reality. The action of taking an oath controls events in the World of Truth. In asking Eliezer to take an oath, Abraham transformed Eliezer from someone who was being influenced into someone who exerts influence.

When we ask the universe for a sign and the sign manifests, and then we react to the manifested sign, we are being influenced, we are not exerting influence, even if the sign comes from the Light. In the case of Eliezer, although he received a sign regarding the soulmate for Isaac, he did not react right away; instead he initiated actions. The power of taking an oath connects with the power of an awakened consciousness.

Why does the Lightforce of the Creator not intervene to end tragic situations? Then the whole world would believe in the existence of the Creator. But we know this will not be the case. We need to understand in our consciousness that the Light provides all the solutions and provides for what we lack. If it is not in our consciousness, then as soon as the lack is provided for we will instantly forget the existence of the Creator.

10 And the servant took ten camels of the camels of his master and departed, taking with him all kinds of good things from his master. And he arose and went to Mesopotamia and to the city of Nahor.

Actions of Intention

Beyond spiritual actions, it is also worthwhile to perform material actions that build channels of communication and to secure a balanced connection to the Lightforce of God. For example, Eliezer used ten camels to ensure a complete connection to the Tree of Life through the Ten Sefirot.

11 He had the camels kneel down near the well outside the city at the time of the evening, the time the women go out to draw water. 12 And he said, "O Lord, God of my master Abraham, I pray You, send me good speed this day, and show kindness to my master Abraham. 13 See, I stand here by the well of water, and the daughters of the men of the city come out to draw water. 14 And let it come to pass that the girl to whom I shall say, 'Let down your pitcher, I pray you, that I may drink,' and she will say, 'Drink, and I will give your camels drink also,' let her be the one You have chosen for Your servant Isaac, and thereby I will know that You have shown kindness to my master." 15 And it came to pass, before he had done speaking, that Rebecca came out, who was the daughter of Bethuel, son of Milca, the wife of Nahor, Abraham's brother, with her pitcher on her shoulder. 16 And the girl was very fair to look at, a virgin; no man had ever known her. And she went down to the well, and filled her pitcher and came up. 17 And the servant ran to meet her and said, "Let me, I pray you, drink a little water from your pitcher." 18 And she said, "Drink, my lord," and she quickly lowered the pitcher to her hand and gave him to drink. 19 And when she had finished giving him a drink, she said, "I will draw water for your camels too, until they have finished drinking." 20 And she hurried and emptied her pitcher into the trough, and ran again to the well to draw water, and drew enough for all his

camels. 21 And the man, without saying a word, watched her closely to see whether the Lord had made his journey successful or not.

Eliezer and Signs from God

Eliezer was looking for signs from God, to ascertain if the Lightforce of God was with him in finding the girl that would be the soulmate of his master's son. The signs were there: Rebecca offered him water to drink and then offered to draw water for his camels as well. It was obvious that the hand of the Lord was present. So why was Eliezer still not certain?

In this section, the Bible wants to teach us that even when we are connected to the Lightforce and are wired right in, nevertheless doubts will spring up. Eliezer's first sign—that the right girl would appear at the well—should have been enough evidence that this was the girl for Isaac. But it was not. The Bible is teaching us that man's natural tendency, as he goes along in life, is to be swallowed up by each and every incident that happens. When a problem arises after things have been going well, we react as if it is all over, and we begin to wonder if God will help. We have seen this throughout history. It appears that God is not always with the people. God was supposedly not there during the destruction of the Temples or the Holocaust. In fact, if we were to investigate the chronicles of history, we would find that the incidences of God's presence are few and far between; it is as if God is almost never there or here. Yet, we continue to go to temple and we continue to pray to God. Anyone who finds themselves in need asks God for help, if they think there is no other alternative, irrespective of religious affiliations. Even the atheist, at times, will ask God for help, and yet, it appears as though God is never around.

This incident at the well, for Eliezer and Rebecca, is a perfect example of God's presence, and yet, Eliezer still questioned. He was in doubt about her lineage, and he wanted to ensure she was not a Canaanite. Our Desire to Receive is so strong that, even if things have been going well for 40 years and suddenly we find ourselves faced with stumbling blocks or periods of lack, we feel that God has abandoned us. Why did God not abandon us all those many years prior to this? If we are wired to the Lightforce, then the problems that seem to come—and they always do in life—are there only to test whether we really believe in God. Do we believe in God when things are great or do we also believe in God when things are not working out the way we believe they should?

Is God playing some kind of game with us? God can bring a person to extreme wealth and then take it away. Does this mean that suddenly God has abandoned them? The answer is that, when things are going well, as in the case of Eliezer, we forget—because the Dark Lord is always there attempting to penetrate our connection with the Lightforce. He wants to bring negativity into our thoughts and into our lives—this is his purpose.

The Dark Lord knows that the only time he can infiltrate people is when things are going pretty well and we have become complacent. If we are healthy, do we appreciate it is the Lightforce that is providing this health or is it just natural that we are healthy? We take it for granted that our health belongs to us and is part of our domain. But the truth of the matter is that nothing is part of our domain. Even when we have it—the health, the wealth, et cetera—it is not part of our domain, it is not our possession. We need to work on our connection, our wiring into the Lightforce, not when things are bad but when things are going well. When things are just great and we are proceeding on schedule, we tell God to take a vacation—maybe even for 40 years. Then in one day, we need God. This is what this portion is about.

Kabbalah is attempting to teach us, to raise our consciousness, raise our awareness, and I am not saying it is easy. The concept is easy, the understanding is simple. We know of people who had everything and lost it overnight. How do these things happen? These things occur to reveal to us that we are not in control or that certainly we do not have control to the extent that we believe we have. I have not said anything here that is beyond comprehension. What makes it so difficult for us to be aware that we need the support of the Lightforce of God? Why do we forget? Rav Shimon bar Yochai says that the moment we forget, we have assumed that the Lightforce is not necessary at that given moment. Is it not part of our expectations, when we are in an automobile on the highway, that we will reach our destination? Why is it expected? In fact, because it is expected, our consciousness goes to sleep, and this is where we abandon the Lightforce—and not the other way around. Even when we read or hear about the statistics of accidents that happen, our default consciousness is that this is about someone else, not us—it is always someone else. This is the Dark Lord working his games on us.

Each day, in a particular prayer of the morning connection, we thank God for all the miracles we did not see. This is not referring to the miracle of just avoiding an accident—which is an obvious miracle. This prayer is for the times when we do not see what could have happened. This prayer is to instill within us a consciousness that we do not abandon God but instead demand of God. God says we can demand all day, and He will be there for us. But the moment we say that, right now, we do not need Him, God moves back. This is the condition of the physical dimension. Then when something happens and we call on Him, after we have kept Him away, we get upset and complain, "God, where are You when I need You most?" And God replies, "You need Me every day. Are you certain with your life every day, are you certain with every aspect of your relationships every day?" The answer is no. This is the power of the Dark Lord, and this is what Eliezer was referring to.

22 And it came to pass, as the camels had finished drinking, that the man took out a gold earring weighing half a shekel, and two bracelets for her hands weighing ten shekels of gold. 23 And said, "Whose daughter are you? Tell me, I pray you, is there room in your father's house for us to lodge in?" 24 And she said to him, "I am the daughter of Bethuel, the son that Milcah bore to Nahor." 25 She said more to him, "We have both straw and fodder enough, and room to lodge in." 26 And the man bowed down his head and worshiped the Lord. 27 And he said, "Blessed be the Lord, God of my master Abraham, who has left destitute my master of His mercy and truth: As for me, the Lord has led me to the house of my master's brethren."

The Pitcher and the 72 Names

When Eliezer's adventures are described, a hidden code appears—the power of the 72 Names of God. The world *kad* ("water jug" or "pitcher") has the numerical value of 24, and it appears in this portion nine times in various combinations, such as "your jug" and "her jug." When we multiply 9 x 24 it equals 216, which is the actual number of letters in the 72 Names of God (3 x 72 = 216). This is another piece of evidence proving that the power to go beyond nature was given to us from the day the world was created.

Rebecca and the Three Column System

Included in this portion is the story of Isaac and his soulmate. It revolves around Abraham sending his servant Eliezer to seek out a wife for Isaac in his father's land. This trusted servant went on a journey and saw a little girl drawing water from a well. He said to himself, "If she will offer me water and give all my camels to drink, then I will know she is the wife for Isaac." This may seem unimportant to anyone who understands the literal Hebrew. However, according to the Midrash, Rebecca was three years old at that time. How was it possible that a three-year-old girl could draw water from the well, let alone also draw enough water for the camels to drink? How is it possible that she is well versed in correct behavior too and agrees of her own free will to go to a far-off land to be married? In this day and age, we find it impossible to comprehend a three-year-old with such abilities. But Kabbalah teaches us that, whenever we look beyond and eliminate physicality, we revolutionize our thinking. When our sages of blessed memory say Rebecca was three years old, they were not referring to her chronological age, they were hinting at her spiritual level. Three indicates Right, Left, and Center. Rebecca was connected to the Three Column System—the complete spiritual system for the revealment of Light in the world. This is why she was fit to be married to Isaac, to give birth to Jacob, and continue in the way of Sarah, our matriarch.

All the descriptions of Eliezer's travels to find Rebecca comprise instructions about the way to find fit partners, whether in marriage, business, or other aspects of life. The power of the soulmate is also revealed in the Haftarah between King David and Batsheva, and not only through Chayei Sarah itself.

28 And the girl ran and told her mother's house about these things. 29 And Rebecca had a brother and his name was Laban, and Laban ran out to the man at the well. 30 And it came to pass, when he saw the earring and bracelets in his sister's hands, and when he heard the words of Rebecca saying, "Thus spoke the man to me," that he came to the man and found him standing by the camels near the well. 31 And he said, "Come in, you who are blessed by the Lord. Why are you standing out here? I have prepared the house and a place for the camels." 32 And the man went into the house, and he unloaded his camels, and gave straw and fodder to the camels, and water to wash his feet and the feet of the men that were with him. 33 And food was set before him to eat, but he said, "I will not eat until I have told you why I am here." And he said, "Speak on." 34 And he said, "I am Abraham's servant. 35 And the Lord has blessed my master greatly, and he has become wealthy. And He has given him flocks and herds, and silver and gold, menservants and maidservants, and camels and donkeys. 36 And Sarah, my master's wife, bore a son to my master in her old age, and he has given him all that he has. 37 And my master made me swear an oath, and said, 'You must not get a wife for my son from the daughters of the Canaanites, in whose land I live, 38 but go to my father's house and to my own kind, and take a wife for my son.' 39 Then I said to my master, 'What if the

woman will not come back with me?' 40 And he replied, 'The Lord, before whom I walk, will send His angel with you and make your journey a success, and you will take a wife for my son from my kind and of my father's house. 41 Then, when you go to my kind, you will be released from this oath even if they refuse to give her to you—you will be released from my oath.' 42 And I came this day to the well, and said, 'O Lord, God of my master Abraham, if You grant success to the journey on which I have come; 43 see, when I stand by the well of water, if the virgin comes out to draw water and I say to her, 'Give me, I pray you, a little water from your pitcher to drink,' 44 and she says to me, 'Drink, and I will also draw water for your camels,'' let her be the one the Lord has chosen for my master's son.' 45 And before I was done speaking in my heart, Rebecca came out, with her pitcher on her shoulder, and she went down to the well and drew water, and I said to her, 'Let me drink, I pray you.' 46 And she quickly lowered her pitcher from her shoulder and said, 'Drink, and I will give your camels drink also.' So I drank, and she made the camels drink also. 47 And I asked her and said, 'Whose daughter are you?' And she said, 'The daughter of Bethuel, son of Nahor, whom Milcah bore to him.' And I put the earring upon her face and the bracelets on her arms, 48 and I bowed down my head and worshiped the Lord and blessed the Lord, the God of my master Abraham, who had

led me on the right road to take my master's brother's daughter for his son. 49 And now if you will deal kindly and truly with my master, tell me; and if not, tell me, so that I may turn to the right hand or to the left."

Abraham's Servant Confronts Negativity

Laban, Rebecca's brother, was a great magician—indeed he was an impersonation of Satan—and also the grandfather of the evil Bilaam. Eliezer knew he would have to confront a great power of negativity before he could remove Rebecca from that place. He repeated to his hosts all the details of the way he met Rebecca because the story makes it clear that Eliezer and Abraham enjoyed the private supervision of the Light. In his story, Eliezer gave a message to Laban and to the rest of his family that they should not try to get in Abraham's way, as they did not stand a chance. Here is an important teaching: Eliezer was a channel for Abraham's power of *chesed*, and therefore was successful—and every one of us who wants to achieve success must be a channel for the energy of *chesed*, the awareness of unity and unconditional love, by connecting to Abraham, our patriarch. Chayei Sarah gives us the means to do this.

50 Then Laban and Bethuel answered and said, "This comes from the Lord; we cannot speak to you bad or good. 51 See, Rebecca is before you; take her and go, and let her become the wife of your master's son, as the Lord has spoken." 52 And it came to pass that when Abraham's servant heard their words, he worshipped the Lord, bowing himself to the earth. 53 And the servant brought out jewels of silver and jewels of gold, and raiment and gave them to Rebecca; he also gave to her brother and to her mother precious things. 54 And they ate and drank, he and the men who were with him, and spent the night there. And they rose up in the morning, and he said, "Send me on my way to my master." 55 And her brother and her mother replied, "Let the girl remain with us a few days, at least ten; after that she will go." 56 And he said to them, "Do not hinder me, seeing the Lord has granted success to my journey; send me on my way so I may go to my master."

Do Not Hold Up the Light

Eliezer said to Bethuel's family that they should not delay him (Beresheet 24:56). This is meant to teach us that, when the Light is with us, we must not hold up the flow or manifestation of it—unless we want to hinder its success. In spite of all the encouraging signs that showed themselves along Eliezer's way, he did not become complacent; he behaved like a professional navigator—he verified the connection with the Light. Eliezer knew it was not enough to be right or wise in life—one also needs the Light.

57 And they said, "We will call the girl and ask her about it." 58 And they called Rebecca and asked her, "Will you go with this man?" And she said, "I will go." 59 And they sent their sister Rebecca on her way, along with her nurse and Abraham's servant and his men. 60 And they blessed Rebecca and said to her, "You are our sister, may you be the mother of thousands of millions; may your seed possess the gates of their enemies." 61 And Rebecca rose and her maids and they mounted the camels and went back with the man. And the servant took Rebecca and went on his way.

Rebecca as a Pure Soul

Laban and Eliezer agreed to ask Rebecca whether she was willing to marry Isaac, and they indeed did everything according to her wishes, even though she was only three years old. How could they rely on the reply of a three-year-old girl? Could they not have waited until she was 18? Did no one ask Isaac's opinion? What we learn from this is that Rebecca was not soiled by all the filth of the Desire to Receive for the Self Alone, so her advice could be taken. This teaches us that a pure and unsullied person can give advice. There are too many "wise" people who think they can give counsel and help others, but only a pure person can do so. Those who give advice are often clever people who may believe they know what is good for others but not what is good for themselves. They would be better off if they took care of themselves instead of giving advice to others. Karen and I do not like to give advice to people because we feel we are not in the same position as Rebecca was when she was three years old. People will always come to those who truly want to give advice. Indeed, when people come to the Kabbalah Centres, they are told they should pave their own way, but that we will assist them in this endeavor.

Rebecca's Age and the Illusion of Physicality

Rebecca's family sent her away with her wet nurse. Do we accept this? Rebecca said that she would travel with a man she had just met on a journey to be married to a man she had never met. I have never found that a three year-old behaves this way. For 3,400 years, people have accepted this story—and this is hard to understand. What are we meant to understand from this story? It is the restoration of the dead, restoring life into something that has expired, a dead kidney, a dead brain, or a clinical death. This is what the Zohar gleans from these seemingly unrelated sections. Abraham bought a cave and buried Sarah there, and then we learn about the process of acquiring a wife for Isaac. This portion reveals that Sarah never died. And the details of Rebecca's age reveal the corruption of the concepts of time, space, and motion.

How old is this physical world? This question has sent the world of science on a collision course with religion. Some say it is a few thousand years old, while science says billions. If dinosaur fossils and geological evidence prove the age of the planet, how can religious notions have any validity? What we have the opportunity to learn here is so profound: Our perception of time, space, and motion has been corrupted. That is what the Bible wants to teach us and that is what we want to draw from this reading.

When we hear that someone died, the inevitable question is: "How old were they?" If the answer is 98, we may say, "Well, they had a long life." Whereas if a person dies at age 21, the natural reaction is: "Oh my God, their whole life was ahead of them." Is time a factor? Does it matter how old a person is when they die? If the deceased was 120, are we to believe there is no reason to cry? Yet, at 21 it is a tragedy. Our concept of time is corrupt, and as long as this corruption remains in our consciousness our thinking will be wrong. If a man is alive at 190 years of age, will people tell him to lie down and die because he is too old? Where are we coming from? Where is our consciousness?

Our values are askew. We believe a handsome man must be good and an ugly man must be bad. What is all advertising about but appearances? Our consciousness is distorted; we have lost the knowledge of what time, space, and motion are all about.

The morning prayers, *Hashem Melech, Hashem Malach, Hashem Imloch* (God rules, God ruled, and God will rule) together with the meditation of the five final Hebrew letters, known by the acronym *Manzepach* (ך.ף.ץ.ן.ם), assist us to eliminate the limitations of time, space, and motion.

62 And Isaac came from the well Lahairoi, for he was living in the south country. 63 And Isaac went out to meditate in the field at dusk, and he lifted up his eyes and saw the camels approaching. 64 And Rebecca lifted up her eyes, and when she saw Isaac, she dismounted the camel. 65 And she asked the servant, "Who is that man in the field coming to meet us?" And the servant said, "It is my master." So she took her veil and covered herself. 66 And the servant told Isaac all the things he had done. 67 And Isaac brought her into the tent of his mother Sarah, and took Rebecca and she became his wife and he loved her; and Isaac was comforted after his mother's death.

Sarah and Rebecca

The Bible says, Rebecca saw Isaac and the servant Eliezer spoke to Isaac and told him all that had transpired. And Isaac brought Rebecca to the tent of his mother Sarah, he takes her and she becomes his wife and he loves her. And now he begins to console himself after the death of his mother. Regarding this section, the Zohar says something very strange but it gives us an insight into how to read and to understand this:

Rav Yehuda said, "SARAH HIS MOTHER" MEANS THAT because the image of Isaac was the same as the image of Abraham, whoever saw Isaac said it was Abraham. Of course, they knew that Abraham begot Isaac, so the image of Rivka [Eng. Rebecca] was exactly the same as the image of Sarah. For that reason it is written, "Sarah his mother."

The images of Isaac and Rivka were exactly the same as the images of Abraham and Sarah. It was apparent that Abraham begat Isaac and Sarah bore Rivka. Rabbi Elazar said, This EXPLANATION is exactly right, but come and behold this secret. Although Sarah died, her image did not leave the house. It remained unseen from the day she died until Rivka came. Once Rivka came, the image of Sarah was seen again, as it is written, "And Isaac brought her into his mother Sarah's tent," but it was seen only by Isaac when he entered the tent. Therefore, "Isaac was comforted after his mother," (Beresheet 24:67) because his mother was seen and chanced before him in the house. Therefore it is not written, "After his mother's death," but rather "after his mother," because she never died for Isaac.
—Zohar, Chayei Sarah 25:249-250

The only one who could see Sarah was Isaac, and "he was comforted after his mother" because she came back to him. When someone dies, there is something called *Shiva* where the family of the deceased is consoled by visitors. The Zohar explains that when a person sits *shiva*, they usually do this in the home of the person who departed because the deceased person is there, and if no one sees the departed person it is not really a consolation. When Isaac and Rebecca walked into Sarah's tent, Isaac was consoled because his mother was there. She came back to him—this is the consolation.

The Zohar continues:

Rav Shimon then discoursed on the difference in verse that is written of Isaac, "And took Rivka, and she became his wife; and he loved her." (Beresheet 24:67) Because it is written that "she became his wife," we should assume that he loved her as all the inhabitants of the world love their wives. What was different here, that made it necessary to add, "And he loved her"? HE ANSWERS, Assuredly the awakening of the love of the male for the female is from the Left COLUMN, as it is written, "His left hand is under my head." (Shir HaShirim 8:3) Darkness, THE LEFT COLUMN, and night, THE NUKVA, are as one, because the Left always arouses love to the Nukva and holds on to her. Therefore, although Abraham loved Sarah, it is not written of him, "And he loved her," but only of Isaac, WHO IS THE LEFT COLUMN OF ZEIR ANPIN. If you say, however, that it is written, "And Jacob loved Rachel," (Beresheet 29:18) THOUGH HE IS NOT OF THE LEFT COLUMN, it is because that side of Isaac was included within him.

—Zohar, Chayei Sarah 25:251-252

What happened here? Why did he love her? When he married her and saw that the presence of Sarah had returned, he knew who Rebecca was. Sarah died only for those who could not see her, although she actually lived.

The Relationship between Isaac and Rebecca

True love is when you feel unity with the individual, not how the chemistry between you can make you feel. I am not saying that chemistry and those other aspects are not important. I do not want to entirely minimize their importance, but what is certain is the way two people feel about a closeness that manifests itself as oneness or true love. A soulmate is a part of you, whether you seem to be compatible or not. First there is a metaphysical aspect—the consciousness— and this is what will bring love.

Isaac took Rebecca for his wife because she was his soulmate. First it was established that they were soulmates and then, that they loved one another. We have to understand that if we do not take our rightful places in life, someone else will. We do not do anyone any favors, because the Creator always fills a place of lack. After Sarah died, Rebecca took her place. The issue of partners exists only recently; in the past no one spoke about partners. Love is when people are in a state of giving to others, even those who they do not know, and not just to family members. Love is when people are invited into homes for sparks to be revealed, to reveal Light in people—only then can there be true love.

Physical and Spiritual Signs

Isaac, like Eliezer, knew the rule about needing the Light, and when Rebecca appeared, Eliezer told him about all of his adventures and all of the signs he received from the Light. Still, Isaac made his own examination because Eliezer's signs were all on the material plane (Beresheet 24:14 & 24), and Isaac's examination was on the spiritual plane. When Rebecca entered Sarah's tent, the *Shechinah*—the Divine Presence, which had disappeared from the tent on the day Sarah passed away—entered with her. In this way, Isaac knew Rebecca was the one who would continue his mother's spiritual path and was therefore suitable to be his wife and the mother of his children.

This story describes the way the spiritual bond between Isaac and Rebecca was formed. Reading this section also allows us to connect with the consciousness of our forefathers and apply the same methodology today. First, "Isaac took Rebecca and she became his wife." Of course, both sides expressed the willingness to create a bond, and they made the bond official, according to customs and law. Then, afterwards, it says "he loved her," which means that out of their common life, the love between them grew and developed.

Desire can be awakened with a first glance but love, union, and the equating of form can only develop out of a common life together and teamwork. Finally, "Isaac was comforted," because the Light they had discovered together filled the space that was left in Isaac's soul after his mother left this world. The numerical value of the root *nachem* (נחם), meaning "to comfort," has the same numerical value as the word *tzach* (צח) "to cleanse," indicating to us that the Light cleansed the space.

Beresheet 25:1 Then again Abraham took a wife, whose name was Keturah. 2 And she bore him Zimran, and Jokshan, and Medan, and Midian, and Ishbak, and Shuah. 3 And Jokshan begat Sheba and Dedan; and the sons of Dedan were the Asshurites, the Letushites, and the Leummites. 4 And the sons of Midian were Ephah, and Epher, and Hanoch, and Abida, and Eldaah. All these were the children of Keturah. 5 And Abraham gave all that he had to Isaac. 6 But to the sons of the concubines which Abraham had, Abraham gave gifts and sent them away from his son Isaac, while he lived eastward, to the land of the east.

The Difference between Kabbalah and the Far Eastern Spiritual Traditions

Before his death, Abraham gave all he had to Isaac but he still had some left over to give as gifts to the sons of his concubines. How was this possible? Why is it important for us to know Ishmael's descendants and his age when he died? What do all these matters have in common? Beresheet 25:6-7 describes the manner in which Abraham passed his inheritance to his offspring while he was still alive. "Abraham gave all that he had to Isaac," tells us that Isaac received Abraham's complete awareness, that is to say his ability to connect with the Sefira of Chesed, beyond Isaac being a vehicle for the Sefira of Gevurah, and the ability to relate to the Sefirot in the complete and balanced context of the Three Column System. This context, which is studied by means of the Zohar, is what enables the activation of the power of resistance, the revealment of Light in a harmonious manner and the ability to control one's destiny.

In contrast, the sons of the concubines only received gifts. The Hebrew word for gifts, *matanot*, is written without the letter *Vav*, (מתנת rather than מתנות), which indicates there was no connection to Zeir Anpin (the Central Column) or Sefira Tiferet (the connection to the Tree of Life). The sons of the concubines were sent eastward, to the land of Kedem. This is the earliest source that connects the people of the Far East with spiritual systems that are based solely on two columns, Left and Right, Yin and Yang (in Chinese Taoism), and light and darkness (Buddhism in India). Because these systems do not have a Central Column, they lack the means of exercising the power of resistance. For this reason, they do not control the forces of nature; they do not have the ability to get out of the influence of the planets and the astrological signs; and they do not have the ability to actualize eternal life and the Resurrection of the Dead.

When we opened up the doors to Kabbalah in Israel, we advertised meditation. At that time, most Israelis were going to Transcendental Meditation. Someone asked if there was any meditation in Judaism. Of course there was not. Finally, we opened up a meditation class, and they came to us. I said at that time that what the Maharishi Mahesh Yogi and the others had brought to the world was necessary, because that was what they had received in the way of a gift from Abraham. This is the way the Zohar describes it.

Although our system is complete, ours is not closed to non-Jews. However, there was a time when this was a necessary component to becoming involved with Kabbalah. So when we came along and said there is meditation in Judaism, it was not so foreign. The Bible tells us that Abraham gave the complete system to Isaac, and that is what we have. I am not saying that the other systems in the Far East are inadequate—they all serve a purpose. Their purpose is to contribute to raising the awareness of humankind. I do not dispute all of the things these different forms of meditation have achieved, including the fact that their practices have medical substantiation. We are discussing the elimination of chaos here, not only from our own lives but, from the lives of everyone in this universe. The Zohar says that the only approach by which we can ultimately bring total contentment and eliminate all suffering from the entire world is through the Zohar itself.

7 And these are the days of the years of Abraham's life which he lived, a hundred and seventy-five years. 8 Then Abraham breathed his last breath and died at a good old age, an old man and full of years; and he was gathered to his people. 9 And his sons Isaac and Ishmael buried him in the Cave of Machpelah, in the field of Ephron, the son of Zohar the Hittite, which is near Mamre; 10 the field which Abraham had purchased from the sons of Heth. There Abraham was buried with his wife Sarah. 11 And it came to pass after the death of Abraham that God blessed his son Isaac, and Isaac lived by the well Lahairoi. 12 Now these are the generations of Abraham's son Ishmael, whom Sarah's maidservant, Hagar the Egyptian, bore to Abraham. 13 And these are the names of the sons of Ishmael, by their names, according to their generations: Nebaioth, the firstborn of Ishmael, and Kedar, and Adbeel, and Mibsam, 14 and Mishma, and Dumah, and Massa, 15 Hadad, and Tema, Jetur, Naphish, and Kedemah. 16 These are the sons of Ishmael, and these are their names, by their towns and by their castles; twelve princes according to their nations.

The Zodiac and Continuity

The passing away of Abraham in this portion enables us to connect to the entirety of his spiritual power, just as we have the ability on the day of the death anniversary of a righteous soul. We must rally our system of spiritual defense to neutralize negative energies around us and connect with the energy of *chesed* or loving kindness.

It is known that each of the twelve signs of the zodiac has a negative and a positive aspect. The positive aspects are ruled by the twelve sons of Jacob, while the negative aspects are ruled by the twelve sons of Ishmael. This section enables us to control all of these ruling ministers and neutralize the negative levels of the zodiac at the root level. This is an additional tool for strengthening our system of spiritual defense and enables us to achieve a much clearer communication with the Light.

Descendants, Satan and the Light

We read in the Mincha connection, "Isaac son of Abraham, and Abraham gave birth to Isaac." Many commentators remark upon this and when the Bible says, "And these are the descendants" it indicates continuity, which is like the power of Ein Sof, the Endless World of the Light, which is the essence of connection to the Tree of Life and the opposite of finiteness and death.

How is it possible to know where we come from and of what our motivation consists? If we ask ourselves before each action whether this action can be classified as giving or as receiving, we can know whether or not we are connected with the Light. When we speak, we generally do not think about the words we utter. Are we like robots in this? The real question is: Are we robots of Satan or robots of the Light? The only difference is intention—whether to give wholeheartedly or merely have influence and be seen only as concerned with how well we speak and how much importance we have.

The power of descendants is the power of continuity but only when we are connected with the Light. The act of giving is a matter of continuity. When a person is not connected with the Light there is no continuity, things do not flow and he or she is a robot of the Satan.

17 And these are the years of the life of Ishmael, a hundred and thirty-seven years, and he breathed his last breath and died, and he was gathered to his people. 18 And they dwelled from Havilah to Shur, near the border of Egypt, as you go towards Assyria. And he died in the presence of all his brethren.

The Arab Nation and Ishmael

Regarding this verse, Rashi explained that the expression "he breathed his last breath" is only used for the righteous. And from this section we learn that Ishmael underwent a process of *teshuvah* (repentance) before his death. Why is it important for us to know this? The answer hurts because it is so pertinent to our times. The Arab nation comes from the offspring of Ishmael, and if the father of the nation was righteous, his sons cannot all be completely evil. Therefore the responsibility for the Israeli-Arab conflict cannot lie only with the Arabs. In fact, the behavior of the Arabs reflects the spiritual evil that has taken residence in the souls of the Israelites. As long as we do not purify ourselves from causeless hatred within us, no real peace will be established in the Middle East or anywhere else in the world.

Sarah's Life, Kiriyat Arba, Jonah, and Resurrection of the Dead

As was said previously, this portion deals with the life of Sarah, and if we look to the Zohar, which is supposed to give us the internal meaning of the portion, we find that it talks about Jonah. What is the connection between Jonah and the life of Sarah? The Zohar says:

"And Sarah's life was a hundred year and twenty year and seven years." (Beresheet 23:1) Rav Yosi opened the discussion with the verse, "So they took up Jonah, and cast him into the sea, and the sea ceased from its raging." (Jonah 1:15) We have to examine this text carefully. Why did the sea rage upon Jonah and not the earth, NAMELY THE NUKVA CALLED EARTH? He was leaving the land, so that the Shechinah would not hover above him. In other words, he was running away from the land of Israel from the secret of the Nukva. If so, why did the sea seize him when he went away, and not the land from which he ran? RAV YOSI ANSWERS THAT the verse was accurate, for the sea resembles the Firmament, and the Firmament resembles the Throne of Glory. For that reason, the sea grabbed him and received him in its midst. He was fleeing from the sea, namely from the prophecy that is drawn from the *Mochin* of the *Nukva*, which is an aspect of the sea. Thus, the sea raged upon him, not the land. He was cast into the sea to return him to the prophecy from which he was fleeing. "So they took up Jonah, and cast him into the sea." We learned that when they cast him into the sea and immersed him to his knees, the sea calmed. When they lifted him, the sea raged. The deeper they immersed him, the calmer the sea became, until he said, "Take me up, and cast me into the sea." (Jonah 1:12) Immediately, "they took up Jonah, and cast him into the sea." When he was thrown into the sea, his soul soared and ascended to the King's throne to be judged. When his soul was returned to him, he entered the mouth of that fish, which died and later came back to life. Come and behold, When a man goes to sleep each night, his soul leaves him to be judged before the King's court. If it merits life, his soul is returned to this world.
— Zohar, Chayei Sarah 1:1-5

Jonah died inside the fish, and the Creator revived him and then revived the fish. The Zohar explains that this story is not referring to an incident where someone dies and one has to purchase a burial site, which is what the biblical portion is dealing with. The Zohar says several things here that are almost impossible to understand, but there is a clue here to which I am alluding. Rav Shimon says that when the *se'ah* is finished, then there is a form of resurrection. This is why this incident with Jonah occurred with the whale—and this is the connection to Sarah.

Se'ah is a measurement of water. The place where we have *se'ah* mentioned in the Talmud and in the Zohar both concern the *mikveh*. The theme of this section of the Zohar is that Sarah is alive. The Zohar is speaking of the Resurrection of the Dead, the dimension in which nothing disappears and why we know that Sarah did not die. Jonah in the water, Sarah and the *se'ah* measurement of water relate to each other. What is the connection?

Rav Abraham Azulai is the Moroccan kabbalist responsible for all of us being able to study the Wisdom of Kabbalah today. It was he who declared, some 400 years ago, that the Age of Aquarius had begun and now everyone is permitted to study Kabbalah. Although this did not happen until the mid-1970s, with the first Kabbalah Centre, which was also a closed place of study initially, just for a select few. Then we opened up the doors to anyone who wants to learn Kabbalah.

In his book *Chesed LeAvraham*, Rav Avraham Azulai discusses the importance of *mikveh*, which I am now going to tie in with Abraham purchasing the field called *Ma'arat haMachpelah* from Ephron for 400 shekels. Here is a story about a business deal supposedly being consummated. Why does Ephron say 400, not 399 or 401? Keep in mind all of these little pieces of information we have just received from the Zohar. Rav Avraham Azulai explains that there are 400 levels of uncleanliness—*Ruach hatuma. Ruach* is a force, and *tuma* is uncleanliness but not from the aspect of being physically dirty—it is spiritual uncleanliness. *Tuma* is chaos. *Tuma* means there is a short-circuit—no energy flow. When there's no energy flow, there is darkness, there is death, and everything that represents chaos—no Light. These *Ruach hatuma* are the forces that create all of the chaos. Therefore, there are 400 levels of chaos in the world. Rav Avraham Azulai says that to remove *Ruach hatuma* we need 40 *se'ah* of water—which is what a *mikveh* is comprised of. As we discussed previously, the Zohar in the story of Jonah also mentions the word *se'ah*, which did not make any sense. What does this have to do with Sarah?

The measurement of one *se'ah* is a 144 average sized eggs, which is a gross of eggs. This is the exact measurement of a *se'ah* of water. The *mikveh*, this place of purification, must contain 40 *se'ah* (144 x 40) equals 5,760. Avraham Azulai also discusses the weight, which is *Yud-Bet dinin*—the exact dimensions are very specific. The removal of this *Ruach hatuma*, the 400 levels of evil, can only be achieved with water. Why? It is like an automobile. When you take away the motor, there is no force left to run it. It is the same idea, says Avraham Azulai. When this force of *tuma* comes in contact with water, it immediately disappears. It is vaporized; it no longer exists. Therefore, the only way to remove these forces is through water. What is the power inherent in water, and why do we need to know of it? The Zohar says that the reality of everything is consciousness. Consciousness determines what goes on. There is nothing but consciousness. The physical reality is illusionary because it comes and goes like the body of a person. When a body that is buried decomposes, is that death? No, because the soul keeps going on. The bodies come and go. They are part of the Illusionary Realm, meaning, today it is here, tomorrow it is gone.

The force of water comes from the level of Chochmah, the highest, purest level of the Lightforce of God. The *Yud* of the Tetragrammaton also represents Chochmah. The Ari shows us the relation between the power of the *mikveh*, which is 144 *se'ah* of water, and the *Yud* of the Tetragrammaton. According to Kabbalah, when we spell out the name of a Hebrew letter it becomes materialized. For instance, the letter *Yud* spelled out is *Yud, Vav, Dalet*, (*Yud* -10, *Vav* - 6, *Dalet* - 4), which adds up 20. When the *Yud* is spelled out using a certain formula, it adds up to 144 because each letter represents a number.

We can make six different combinations of the letter *Yud, Vav, Dalet*:

> *Yud, Vav, Dalet*
> *Yud, Dalet, Vav*
> *Vav, Dalet, Yud*
> *Vav, Yud, Dalet*
> *Dalet, Yud, Vav*
> *Dalet, Vav, Yud*

The total numerical value of these six combinations is 6 x 20=120. The total number of letters is 3 x 6=18, which is an additional force beside the total numerical value. Avraham Azulai explains that when we add the value of the six combinations (120), with the total number of letters (18) and the number of combinations (6), we get 144: 120+18+6=144. First we have the parts and then we have the sum of the parts. Each letter is an embodiment of these parts.

We now see that 144 is the force of the letter *Yud*, metaphysically as well as physically because we can now see where the original idea of gross came from. Gross represents a unit; 144 is not just 12 x 12, it is the force of 144 eggs. What emerges is that, if 40 *se'ah* of water are required to remove 400 *Ruach hatuma*, each *se'ah* removes 10 levels of *tuma*. Therefore, the measurement of *se'ah* is likened to the letter *Yud*, whose numerical value is 10. Just as there are the 10 aspects of the Lightforce, there are also 10 aspects of the Dark Lord. Everything in this world has a balance, a counterpart—good and evil. If we make use of the Lightforce, then we can eliminate the Dark Lord. How do we do that? First of all, according to the Zohar, with the knowledge that is required. If one wants to be healed, he or she must instill a concentration of consciousness. Without that, there must be a recurrence. This already has been established. Science says consciousness is the reason why when two people have the same ailment, one can recover and the other one does not.

Rav Avraham Azulai says that in every ailment, in every sickness, there are 400 levels of the Dark Lord called *Ruach hatuma*. The measurement of 40 *se'ah* has the power to remove all of these 400 levels that are included in every disease, in every uncleanliness, or wherever the Dark Lord has latched on.

What is all this build-up, and why does water have this power? In the year 5760, the Zohar says, from the verse in Vayikra 26:6, there will be the removal of the forces of *tuma*. There will be three Resurrections of the Dead: First, there will be the resurrection of the dead Israelites in Israel; then the resurrection of the dead Israelites outside of Israel; the third resurrection will involve all the nations of the world. Now we can understand everything that is mentioned and all of the questions that we raised.

The Zohar asks why is the place called Kiriath Arba (City of Four), which is Hebron? It is because we are discussing the Tetragrammaton, which is made up of four letters. Some say that the reason Hebron was called Kiriath Arba is because there are four couples buried there: Adam and Eve, Abraham and Sarah, Isaac and Rebecca, Jacob and Leah. Hebron comes from the word *chibur*, meaning "comes together," indicating that this is the place that is unified.

As we mentioned previously, how the Bible describes Sarah's name is unique. Sarah's life had within it a connection to Keter, Chochmah, Binah—the seed and totality of everything in unity. Sarah also connected to the Seven Lower Sefirot of fragmentation and separation. Because Sarah's life combined all of the Sefirot in Hebron, in her there was no fragmentation.

The Zohar says that death is an illusion. The people buried in the Cave of Machpelah represent how the Resurrection of the Dead can come about. Adam and Eve, Abraham and Sarah, Isaac and Rebecca, Jacob and Leah are not dead—they never died. They still live there today. When the Bible discusses the death of Abraham and Jacob, it does not say they died; the words used are "they were gathered."

At a funeral today, when the earth is placed on the coffin and it is not out of sight, who is really out of sight of whom? Since we live in a world of illusion, we are living in a world of fragmentation, meaning we think the person in the coffin is gone. This is part of the consciousness of living in the world of illusion. But, by the same token, the person who is being buried is looking at us and now saying, "You people are living in the world of illusion. I no longer am." This whole exchange of consciousness is taking place as the person is being taken away from this realm. When Abraham was lowered into the grave, it was indicating that the world of fragmentation was gone. The Bible says *vayechi chayei Sarah*. This tells us that she lived, and these are the years of her living. She never died. Almost the entire Zohar on the portion of Chayei Sarah discusses Resurrection of the Dead. Resurrection of the Dead means more than just meeting up with our old relatives; it also means *bila hamavet lenetzach*, that death no longer takes place.

When Abraham purchases a burial place for Sarah, we understand from the Zohar that this section is not dealing with how to purchase a piece of property. Even the name Ephron, which comes from the Hebrew word *efer* (ashes), indicates something more than someone negotiating with Abraham. Ephron represents the Dark Lord. When Abraham gave Ephron the 400 shekels, the ownership of the place of unity transferred to Abraham. This is a story about removing the ownership of the Dark Lord, the 400 forces of *tuma*, from our presence. Of course, we have to also behave like Sarah; we cannot keep stealing and lying, and doing all of the things we should not be doing. But when we want to start with a clean slate, what do we do with all of these forces of *tuma* we have accumulated? Avraham Azulai advises us to use the *mikveh*, which can remove these 400 levels of *tuma*. When Abraham gave Ephron the 400 shekels, he was removing Ephron (the Dark Lord) from himself. This story of the sale of the burial plot was to remove the influence of the Dark Lord and to have *techiat hamatim* or the "death of death and restoration of life." Avraham Azulai says that the Resurrection of the Dead will begin in the year 5760, and it will occur in stages. He also explains that immersion in the *mikveh*, with its minimum of 40 *se'ah* of water, creates a form of Resurrection of the Dead because of the removal of the force of *tuma*. There is nothing as powerful as the mikveh we can do that can equal the removal of the Dark Lord.

The Zohar explains that when Ephron said, "Listen, my lord, what is this 400 between me and you?" what he is in essence saying is that the difference between me and you is 400. The difference between life and death, illness and health is 400. The Zohar says that 400 worlds separate us from the Garden of Eden. It is important that we learn and study so we can receive the energy by which we can have the proper consciousness for whatever it is we have to do in the removal of the Dark Lord, wherever there is chaos. *Mikveh* is certainly one of these steps. Scanning the Zohar is another, which is why we recommend that everyone, at the minimum, scans the Zohar if they cannot read it. With consciousness, we speed up the process. This is why the Zohar is discussing the life of Sarah and not the death of Sarah in the portion of Chayei Sarah.

Conclusion: The Path to Blessings

The portion of Chayei Sarah is 105 verses long, and the numerical value of the name Yehoyada (יהוידע) is 105. As we mentioned previously, Yehoyada was a High Priest who lived his entire life in Jerusalem, but was buried in a riverbed in Safed, access to which is very difficult. Why? Because only in that place can the energy connected to the soul of Yehoyada be revealed. What is this energetic essence? The message Yehoyada gave to the world was simple and straight-forward: To reach the goal, one has to undergo difficulties. To gain merit, one has to put forth effort. This is the way Isaac gained Rebecca, and it is the only way we will gain health, a worthy spouse, and success in life.

BOOK OF BERESHEET:

Portion of Toldot

PORTION OF TOLDOT

Beresheet 25:19 And these are the generations of Isaac, the son of Abraham. Abraham became the father of Isaac, 20 and Isaac was forty years old when he married Rebecca, daughter of Bethuel the Aramean from Padanaram, the sister of Laban the Aramean.

Dealing with the Bible

The Zohar says:

> "And these are the generations of Isaac...." (Beresheet 25:19) Rav Chiya opened the discussion with the verse, "Who can utter the mighty acts of the Lord? Who can declare all His praise?" (Tehilim 106:2) Come and behold, when the Holy One, blessed be He, wished to create the world, He did so according to the Torah. And every act that the Holy One, blessed be He, used to create the world was done according to the Torah. This is the meaning of, "then I was by him, as a nursling, and I was daily his delight." (Mishlei 8:30) Do not pronounce it as "a nursling," (Heb. *amon*) but rather "a craftsman" (Heb. *uman*), BECAUSE IT WAS A TOOL FOR HIS CRAFT.
> —Zohar, Toldot 1:1

This discussion in the Zohar is strange for several reasons. We are talking here about the Creator. Did He need the letters of the Bible to reflect upon to permit Him to create the world? The Creator has the power to create the world, all of its inhabitants, and all that it

129

contains. What does the Zohar mean that He did so according to the Bible?

The Zohar continues:

> When He wanted to create man, the Torah said to him, "If man is created, he will sin, and you will punish him. Would not Your handwork then be in vain? After all, he will not be able to endure the punishment." The Holy One, blessed be He, replied, "I created repentance before I created the world. IF HE WILL SIN, HE WILL BE ABLE TO REPENT AND BE FORGIVEN." When the Holy One, blessed be He, created the world and created Adam, He said to it, "World, world, you and your nature are based solely upon the Torah, and for that reason I created man in you, to be occupied with dealing with the Torah. And if he does not DEAL WITH THE TORAH, I will return you to chaos. Everything is for man." This is the meaning of the verse, "I have made the earth, and created man upon it." (Yeshayah 45:12) The Torah proclaims to men to be occupied with and endeavor in the study of the Torah, but no one lends an ear.
> —Zohar, Toldot 1:2

Here it says the Bible spoke to the Creator and to men. Most people who read the Torah Scroll, even on Shabbat or on the holidays, do not hear the Scroll speak—although some do feel this connection. If the purpose of Creation is so that man can return to make our *tikkun* (spiritual correction) because of previous lifetimes of sins, then why does the Torah Scroll ask the Creator, "Why create man, if he is going to sin?" In other words, based on the reincarnation principle, is this not what we came to accomplish in this world? The Zohar here teaches us that this world was created for the purpose of free will—to permit humankind to make a choice—and in this way we can achieve correction. If the consequence for murder and stealing came in an instant, who would murder, who would steal? Where would the free will be to choose not to do so? Therefore, retribution could not come immediately; there would have to be a point whereby an individual could steal and think they got away with it. The opportunity to commit transgressions is part of Creation. So what did the Torah Scroll mean when it said to the Creator, "If man will sin then it is as if Your Creation served no purpose."?

Why was Adam told not to eat from the Tree of Knowledge? Was this because of a doctrine? This is what you do, and this is what you do not do. No. Within Creation there was a frame of reference in place—free choice and self-determination. People would have the choice. Adam would have the choice to stay connected to the Tree of Life Reality, where there was no framework of evil, or he could eat from the Tree of Knowledge. If the Creator did not want Adam to have a choice, He would not have created the Tree of Knowledge in the first place. The Creator established the Tree of Knowledge to provide humankind with free choice. That said, if free will was the reason for Creation—the original Big Bang in the Ein Sof (Endless World)—so that there would no longer be Bread of Shame, then why is the Torah asking of the Creator, "How can You create the world on this basis?" What was the motivation behind the question? And what is meant by the Creator's response: "I created teshuva (repentance)." How does this answer the question that the Bible raised?

Conventional religion regards teshuva (repentance) as saying, "I'm sorry." But if you step on someone's toe and say, "I'm sorry," in what way do you relieve the pain you inflicted? The Creator has provided a system of teshuva to permit us to wipe out our transgressions.

The reason we suspect these questions are valid is because at some point in our lives, we have been conditioned to believe that the creations of the Creator must do His bidding because it is good for us. However, this is not the case. In fact, it is the other way around. Creation seems not to be for our benefit but rather for the Creator's benefit. This is a completely new way of looking at things because this would mean that God created the world for some benefit that might accrue to Him.

Rav Shimon will be taking this direction, and we will shortly get to that, but first I want us to see how the questions raised by Rav Shimon provide us with an entirely different perspective of what the Bible is all about. We all know the importance of studying the Bible. Those who are religious have accepted that it is important to study the Bible. Although I would say from my experience that, when it comes to study of the Bible, there are a great many religious people who are as far removed from it as irreligious people who have no connection whatsoever.

The phrase used by the Creator is: "This world will be sustained by those who are *asuk ba Torah*." The Bible does not say those who will *study* Torah, or those who will *live* by the Torah but rather those who will be *asuk* with the Bible. *Asuk* means "to deal." What does *dealing* with the Bible mean? When we deal with a situation, we come to grips with that situation and make use of that situation. The Zohar says that the world functions in a harmonious way when we *deal* with the Bible, not if we *study* it.

And yet what does all this have to do with the portion of Toldot—with the generations of Isaac, the son of Abraham? Why does the Zohar place this particular aspect of Creation here in this section? We have learned in many other places in the Zohar that the problem was not the created being but that there was something the Creator faced. This condition did not create a lack or deficiency within the Creator since, from a kabbalistic point of view, the Creator is one thing—a force that makes everything move. We call this force the Lightforce of the Creator. It is the energy in electricity. It is the energy that moves the motor in an airplane. Every movement is driven by some internal force that is beyond the physical entity. This force exists within the physical body, and it disappears at death. At death, the body stops moving because there is no longer something internal that motivates the body to move.

There are two parts—the Lightforce of the Creator, and the physicality or the vessel that makes this Lightforce become evident, become manifested. The Lightforce of the Creator is the internal force that motivates the soul to move and think; and it makes the body appear to be thinking. Everything, even inanimate objects, has an energy-intelligence; there is an internal force within. Thanks to the understanding of quantum physics, we know that there is life within a table; ninety-nine percent of the table is atoms, which contain beautiful movement.

The Creator had one thought, and that thought was to share. The Creator becomes revealed because of this internal characteristic of sharing. Everything in this universe also desires to become revealed. The way that something of a metaphysical nature becomes revealed is, fortunately or unfortunately, through a physical corporeal entity. Without a body, the soul cannot reveal itself. Without a physical aspect, the Lightforce of the Creator cannot reveal Itself. The Zohar states that the purpose of Creation was not for the benefit of humankind but rather because the Desire and Thought of Creation is to share. The manner in which the Lightforce could extend Itself in sharing was in creating a vessel, by which there would be a full expression of the Lightforce. Because if there is no vessel—a body, a table, a cup—there would never be an expression of the Lightforce.

The Lightforce is not expressed unless there is a body. A soul may be hovering about, but if that soul does not become manifest within a body there will never be an expression or a manifestation of that Lightforce. Thus for His Desire to Share to become manifested, the Creator created many things, one of which is humankind. Humanity is the channel by which the Lightforce could become expressed. Creation is for the sole purpose that the Creator could extend Itself.

In the Study of Ten Luminous Emanations, Volume 1, we learn that the Lightforce is of a positive nature and that everything of a positive nature wishes to expand, wishes to move out from within the confines of itself to become manifest. The internal characteristic of a good person is to share. This is the very nature of a good person. This is the sole reason things became manifest; and this is why the world was created. Humankind was not created so that we can follow the Torah. The purpose of the Creation, including the creation of humanity, is to make manifest the Lightforce of the Creator. This is the state Adam was in before the sin—in the realm of the Tree of Life. When Adam looked at the Tree of Life, he was satiated as if having eaten a full meal, and he did not need to rid his body of waste because he connected with the internal Lightforce. When we eat, we still retain a certain amount of strength from the food, however the physicality of it is excreted. The feeling of satiation does not come from the physical corporeal aspect of the food, since that disappears, that leaves us.

The Talmud says that the soul is a part of the Creator. It is like a stone that has been separated from the mountain. The internal essence of the stone is the same as the mountain from which it was separated. The soul, relative to the body, has the internal characteristic of the Creator—the Lightforce—therefore the Creator is within all of us. If the Lightforce is not present there is no motivation, even at its lowest level—like lifting a cup. A dead person cannot lift a cup because the Lightforce of the Creator no longer exists; it has left the body. When a tree is uprooted it dies because the Lightforce within it has disappeared. There is only one Lightforce, that of the Creator.

What happens with decay? Physical decay occurs when an entity has become separated from its internal Lightforce. It will ultimately revert back to atoms and disappear. A physical table, for example, is only a conduit for the Lightforce of the Creator. Anything that is a channel has a fixed lifespan. It lasts for so many years, and eventually disintegrates and returns to where it came from or it becomes fossilized like a skeleton, which does not disintegrate.

There is less of the Lightforce in a table than a tree because the table has a lesser intensity of intelligence. Yet both have the same atoms, which are intelligences. The human body consists of ninety-nine percent of atoms. And an atom is made up of three thought energy-intelligences: proton (Desire to Share), electron (Desire to Receive), and neutron (the element that connects both). It is the physical nature—one tenth of one percent—that puts these unrevealed atoms into a revealed state.

Although we must comply with the universal laws and principles of the physical world, this does not negate the fact that, on another level, we can alter nature—depending of course on one's consciousness. Firewalkers walk on hot coals and experience no pain or burning. Under "normal" circumstances, flesh and fire do not go together. The fire wants to consume the flesh. There is a requirement of some element that can bring these two aspects together. The same is true in the case of fire and water. Fire wants to extinguish the water and water wants to extinguish the fire. We maintain balance between the two by using another element—a pot—in which to cook the water. The water is affected by the fire; it has been touched by the fire but not consumed by it. One does not cancel out the other because a Central Column—the third element—can maintain both.

Fire has the internal energy of expansion. It can warm a home, or it can burn a house. That same fire can destroy or create. The difference is that in the case of creating heat, the fire has been confined. With regard to the firewalker, he or she is able to take control of the 1 Percent Reality. With a meditative consciousness they access the 99 Percent Reality: *You are fire. I know your nature is to burn me. It is your instinct to devour whatever comes in contact with you. Well, I am going to confine you so that you will remain in your capacity of heat. I do not cancel you out but I confine you.*

It is like a pot confining the fire so that it will not immediately dry out the water. The pot maintains an equilibrium. Like Adam, firewalkers connect to the ninety-nine percent of reality, so that the fire of those hot coals will not burn their skin.

Although we are conditioned to think that we have no power with the mind, we are beginning to realize this is not the truth. The mind is an incredible instrument, and with this knowledge we begin to understand what the Zohar is addressing.

The Creator looked to the Torah because the Torah is the blueprint of Creation—similar to the blueprint of a building. There must be a blueprint because there are many different thought energy-intelligences that comprise this universe. The blueprint combines all of them and makes them into one unified whole.

Creation means that something not there before becomes created. When someone starts a new business, do they create something new or do they put together elements that are already in existence? It is the same with our body. Though it is a channel for the expression of the Lightforce of the Creator, it is minor in relation to the entire universe.

When the Creator created this world, He used the channels of the twenty-two Hebrew letters of the *Alef Bet*, whose importance is stressed by the Zohar. From the *Sefer Yetzirah* ("Book of Formation"), written by Abraham the Patriarch, we learn that every planet was created by virtue of a Hebrew letter. For example, the letter *Gimel* (ג) created the planet Jupiter. The letter *Resh* (ר) created the planet Mercury.

When the Creator reflected on the Torah, He reflected on the letters and made use of these letters as channels to create that vast expanse of space including this Earth, and including humankind, just as He makes use of a body to permit the soul to express itself. Yet, while Creation might have been for the total benefit of the Creator, we cannot deny that the Vessel does experience something. When the Torah Scroll said to the Creator: "You need man, but what was the purpose?" Man himself says, "I will do You a favor, Creator, I agree to serve as a channel, so that You can become expressed." But there is more to this because humankind will ultimately enjoy it as well, so we cannot say that Creation is just for the Creator. A Rolls Royce may have been created to function, and while we may be doing a service to the Rolls Royce by driving it, we also receive some pleasure as well. When we purchase something, we make that inanimate object become manifest. We are the channel by which this object now becomes operable. It is the same way as atoms in the air: as long as they are not contained, theoretically they have no purpose—they do not become manifest, they do not become expressed.

The power of atoms is that they are indestructible, and because they are thought energy-intelligences we can direct them with our mind. We must not treat atoms as something of a physical nature but rather as an intelligence that has understanding. The atom has a Desire to Receive, a Desire to Share, and a Desire to Restrict. If we can connect mentally to the consciousness of these atoms, they will do whatever we want. They will conform. Everything throughout the universe is a result of humankind's activity.

The Torah Scroll expressed the following: "Man is necessary because there is no other way that You, the Creator, can express Yourself." Man, in effect, makes everything move. And it is true that there is a need of both good and evil because without evil there would be no free choice. However, what if man should create an *aveira*? The word *aveira*, usually translated to mean "sin," actually means a severance of the relationship between man and the Lightforce of the Creator. Thus, in the case of an *aveira*, the Lightforce cannot be manifested. The internal characteristic of stealing, hatred, or murder is a Desire to Receive for Oneself Alone; there is no quality of sharing in these actions. The Desire to Receive creates disunity between the perpetrator and the Lightforce, which is the essence of sharing. The Torah asked why create this channel—man—if, from the beginning, there is the possibility that man will ultimately make this severance. God answered that He created the technology of *teshuvah* (repentance) to counter this severance. Many understand repentance to mean, "I am sorry." But if a person steals the last loaf of bread from a widow with eight children to feed, and then returns to say, "I have eaten the bread. I do not have it to give you but please forgive me," has the request for forgiveness restored everything back to its original condition? No. To understand what repentance means, and how we can repair the damage that we cause, let us examine the word *teshuvah*. The Hebrew word *tashuv* means "to return," and the word *teshuvah*—*tashuv-Hei*—means "to go back to a new future." But where do we go back to?

From this section of the Zohar, we see that *teshuvah* existed before Creation. We discussed earlier that, before the sin, Adam lived in the Tree of Life Reality; if he wanted an apple, he simply looked at the apple and was satiated. He did not connect with the physicality but to the ninety-nine percent of the fruit. The Creator created *teshuvah*—the technology that can bring us back to a new future—to create another consciousness. When we do repentance, it is not enough to say, "I'm sorry." We literally have to go back and create a new future. In other words, the man who stole that loaf of bread consists of two parts: here is a one tenth of one percent or one percent called the physical reality, and there is another reality called the 99 Percent, the Tree of Life Reality.

When we speak of *teshuvah*, we are going back to the time when Adam lived in the Tree of Life Reality. *Teshuvah* is a time travel capsule, and when we go back in time, our consciousness is not the same consciousness—we become someone else because we are in another frame of reference. We are not the person that did a prior negative action because that physical aspect, which once was us, is no longer us. This time capsule was created before Creation because Creation already means the beginning of the physical reality. To do real repentance, we need to go back to the time before physicality existed—to the consciousness level of Zeir Anpin, where we are no longer governed by the physical reality of Malchut, where chaos exists. In other words, there are parallel universes with tracks already laid out. When we connect to the universe of Zeir Anpin, we are on another track of the future. We can move from one parallel universe to the other, right here, right now.

If someone approaches me and says: "Rav, I saw you on 42nd Street and Third Avenue at 12 o'clock," and I was in Mexico City at that hour, could it have been me? The answer, from a kabbalistic point of view, is that I could conceivably have been thinking about being on 42nd and Third Avenue at that exact moment and this person perceived the 99 Percent Reality.

Quantum physics posits that everything is affected by everything else. If we take this time capsule back, it is as if we never stole or did the negative action to begin with. However, it is also important to understand that it does not pay to steal because all that we get is the physicality of that which we stole—the one tenth of one percent of the thing. We cannot connect to the 99 Percent, the Lightforce within it. Stealing is the Desire to Receive for Oneself Alone, thus there is a severance of the affinity with the internal Lightforce, and the person stealing has no connection to that Light. All they connect to is the 1 Percent Illusionary Reality.

The Zohar brings up this concept in the section of Toldot, in regard to Abraham and Isaac, because the Bible is not referring to the physical Abraham and Isaac—since this is the part we consider illusionary. Abraham and Isaac were individuals who encapsulated the energy forces of Chesed (Right Column) and Gevurah (Left Column), and they brought the control of these thought energy-intelligences. When the Zohar discusses "Gevurah of the Creator," it is not referring to "strength," but to mastering, controlling energy forces that are around us. There is nothing real in this world except atoms, which keep living on after we have physically gone. Abraham, Isaac, and Jacob were the first channels for the energies found in the atom: proton (Chesed), electron (Gevurah), and neutron (Tiferet). They are called chariots because they brought down these potential energy forces into our hands (Malchut), so we could make use of them. These were not ordinary people. They were given the art of how to make use of the Hebrew letters—the *Alef Bet*—and therefore control the movement of atoms.

We have to deal with the 1 Percent Reality because this is where the aspect of restriction comes into play. Everything is here now. Tomorrow is here now. We can either permit the 1 Percent to govern us and thereby not perceive things beyond the here and now, or we can do *teshuvah*, which is Restriction—we restrict ourselves from doing that negative action again. Repentance is internalization. Every situation is an illusion, which is why we teach that, according to Kabbalah, we cannot blame anyone for doing anything to us. No one ever stole from anyone, no one can ever hurt someone else. Even if it appears as if the other person has initiated some form of pain or has stolen, it is never someone else.

The Son of Abraham

The word *toldot* means "generations and children." The Bible begins by first telling us about the children of Isaac and then informing us that Isaac is the son of Abraham. This is followed by the words, "Abraham became the father of Isaac." Why does the Bible feel it necessary to repeat the fact that Abraham is the father of Isaac?

Most of the commentary on the Bible is in Hebrew, and you can see the commentators struggle to find meaning because some of the answers they give are not clear. To help us understand the explanations on a superficial level, Rashi (Rav Shlomo Yitzchaki, 1040 – 1105) explains that when Abraham went to Egypt, he was afraid of King Abimelech. Sarah was very beautiful, and Abraham was concerned that King Abimelech would want her. So Abraham told Sarah to say that she was his sister and not his wife. He understood that people would say, when she gave birth to Isaac, that the child was the son of Abimelech and not Abraham. Rashi explains that the Bible repeats that Abraham is the father of Isaac as Isaac looked exactly like Abraham.

The Past and Future are Here Now

Rashi also explains that instead of immediately describing the generations of Isaac, the Bible twice states that Abraham is Isaac's father. The Zohar explains that this is to communicate the notion that yesterday and tomorrow are here and now. The Zohar says this 2,000 years ago, and now I can say it because modern physics agrees. Those who view the Bible literally will be stuck trying to understand the story.

It seems that all we know about is the present, to whatever extent we can grasp that idea. If we want to be mired in society's notions of reality, we will be stuck in illusion. This is the trap of the Satan, the trap of the illusionary world. When we look at a person, do we think they exist? They represent ninety-nine percent of a physical nature. The future is already here, but we cannot accept this unless we believe there is such a thing as tomorrow. With this understanding, we can now begin to comprehend what the Bible meant by discussing the generations of Isaac.

Resurrection of the Dead and the End of the Exile

In this portion, we have the whole of humanity's history from the beginning to the end. This is the reason the Bible states "these are the generations of Isaac, son of Abraham," and not "these are the generations of Isaac, Jacob." The Bible is not referring to a succession from a father to son—Abraham to Isaac, Isaac to Jacob—but rather discussing the succession of all the generations, the development of everything that will ever happen.

The Zohar explains that Toldot is about Resurrection of the Dead and the Exile. The Zohar asks why it is important to know why he was named Isaac and who his father was. And it answers that the name Yitzchak (Hebrew for Isaac) comes from the Hebrew word *tzechok*, meaning "laughter." God gave this name to Isaac to indicate how we can have happiness in our life. Isaac reveals a double-edged sword. On one hand Isaac represents desire—drawing pleasure. And without desire, there is nothing. Yet because he draws desire, he also draws the problem. The Bible says, "These are the generations of Isaac, the son of Abraham." What is Abraham? Abraham is the soul. Isaac is the body. There are two desires: There is the desire of the soul—the Desire to Share—that comes from Abraham and the desire of the body—the Desire to Receive—that comes from Isaac. The Bible tells us that Abraham gave birth to Isaac to indicate to us that within Isaac, whose essence is the Desire to Receive, there is also a Desire to Share that comes from Abraham. Abraham gave birth to Isaac—to happiness, and happiness takes place within us when there is a Desire to Receive for the Sake of Sharing.

From the Zohar we learn that the four sides of the world gather together, and that from the four one spirit would emerge to reestablish the body. Adam was created from the four spirits. The Zohar does not say worlds here but uses the words *arba Ruchot*, meaning "four spirits," which are either the four Sefirot—Chesed, Gevurah, Tiferet, and Malchut, or Chochmah, Binah, Tiferet, and Malchut—*Yud*, *Hei*, *Vav*, and *Hei*. The Zohar does not say "with four" but "from the four," will emerge that one spirit. The four spirits will not become one body but rather the body will emerge from the four when they will be unified. What does "when they will be unified" mean? How will they become unified? They will become unified when we, humankind, create unity. But because there is hatred in the world, everything is separated. This is why the four spirits do not bring about Resurrection of the Dead. If we create unity among ourselves, we create unity in every aspect of the cosmos, in all of the forces that have become separated by the sin of Adam. At the time of the Holy Temple, all the forces were one unified whole.

The Zohar says that this is the spirit that will build. It is the force that is there at birth. This is the spirit that brings in a body the need to eat and drink. A dead body does not need to eat or drink. The

Zohar and the Talmud ask: What is the difference between the time we are living in now and the days of the coming of the *Mashiach* (Messiah), and why are people worried about this? We say we would like Mashiach to come but do we know what this means? Both the Zohar and the Talmud say the only difference is that, upon the coming of *Mashiach*, we will not be mortgaged to Malchut, the limitations of our physical world. We, and not the body, will have control. How are we mortgaged to Malchut? We have to eat and drink to stay alive. Therefore, we are not independent; we are mortgaged to the body. When we have a Desire to Receive for the Sake of Sharing it will lead us to control our bodies, but if we have a Desire to Receive for Oneself Alone then we have to eat—the body is in control. When *Mashiach* comes we will not be dependent on whatever the body wants. In other words, we will direct the body. Rabbi Akiva experienced *Mashiach* because he was divorced from his body; it had no influence over him. When he would sit down to eat, he would say to his body, "I know, you want to eat so, go ahead and eat. I will wait for you until you are finished."

The Zohar asks what the difference is between the time we live in and that of the Resurrection of the Dead—when there will be a restoration and limbs and organs will grow back. I had not understood this section of the Zohar until recently. The Zohar says that what will make the difference is spiritual cleansing and having the comprehension of knowing that this is what is taking place. Resurrection of the Dead is not waiting for God to bring it. There is no such concept. What is holding up the Resurrection of the Dead from becoming a reality is the fact that we do not have the information. The Zohar says that not only the information but also our use of that information will bring about the Resurrection. As we begin to understand that everything we are going through, in the way of pain or suffering, is not pain and suffering but rather it is cleaning away the garbage that we created last year, last lifetime. And also that when we have pain, we say "thank you" because we understand that this pain is taking away a part of the garbage that is still around.

If we still feel pain as pain, we hold back the Resurrection of the Dead from occurring because we are recognizing that there is such a thing as pain, and pain only exists in the world of the Tree of Knowledge Good and Bad. In the Tree of Life Reality there is no pain. Take a woman who used to wash clothes by hand, before there were washing machines. Although this was hard work, the clothes became clean. She did not complain if the water was too cold or her hands hurt. She wanted to have clean clothes; that was the objective. It is the same way when we have pain. If we are suffering when we have pain, then we strengthen and give power to the world of the Tree of Knowledge Good and Bad. It is important for us to know and understand that if we complain and are unhappy, we are living in the Tree of Knowledge Reality and are holding back the Resurrection of the Dead. If we understand that the pain is happening so that now we will be purer, and we use all the kabbalistic tools—the 72 Names of God, Ana Beko'ach, Tikkun HaNefesh, and all the many others—this is Resurrection of the Dead.

We must always remember that, if we want to be part of Resurrection of the Dead, we have to have these two ideas, no matter what the problem we face—whether it is in business, family, or health. If we do not treat it as a cleansing then we are mortgaged to the Tree of Knowledge, and we have to go through the same thing again. This is foolish. If it is happening, we are experiencing some cleansing, so we should get rid of it. But how do we get rid of the pain and suffering? When we tell ourselves that this pain is cleaning out something, that we know will never come back again, then we remove that problem. At the moment the Romans began peeling of his skin with an iron comb, Rabbi Akiva felt the pain for the first minute because he knew he was one of the ten brothers that sold Joseph into slavery and that this was happening not to give him pain but to wash out something that had to be cleaned. After that, his soul left his body and he felt no more pain.

Abraham and Isaac: Chesed and Gevurah

The Zohar says:

> THE SCRIPTURE READS, "And Isaac was forty years old when he took Rivka for a wife." (Beresheet 25:20) Why is Isaac's age given here? Why does it say he was forty years old when he married Rivka? HE BEGAN HIS ANSWER BY SAYING THAT Isaac was included within north and south, which are fire and water, and was then forty years old when he took Rivka. Further, the text, "As the appearance of the bow," (Yechezkel 1:28) means THAT RIVKA HAD "THE APPEARANCE OF THE RAINBOW," WHICH IS green, white, and red, WHICH ARE CHESED, GEVURAH AND TIFERET OF NUKVA. She (the Nukva) was three years old when he seized it, when he took Rivka, THAT IS HE MARRIED HER. And he sired a son when he was sixty, WHICH WAS AFTER ATTAINING THE SIX SEFIROT, CHESED TO YESOD so that he would properly sire Jacob who, as the issue of a man of sixty years, held on to all THE SIX SEFIROT and became a whole man.
> —Zohar, Toldot 2:15

The portion of Toldot opens with the verse: "And these are the generations of Isaac the son of Abraham." It then says that Isaac was 40 years old when he married Rebecca. The Zohar, in the portion of Toldot, asks a clear question: What is the significance of 40, and why do we need to know his age? The answer of the Zohar is extensive in that it explains the manner in which spiritual energy works and flows. Isaac is Left Column, Gevurah (Judgment), while Abraham is Right Column, Chesed (Loving kindness). Abraham's Chesed balances out Isaac's Gevurah, meaning that Abraham's Right Column energy had dominion over Isaac's Left Column energy.

In the Ein Sof (Endless World) there was Light and Vessel, (plus and minus). The vessel draws energy (Left Column) and the Light shares (Right Column). Everything that came into existence after the Ein Sof follows this same pattern of Right and Left because no force in this world can operate without a plus and a minus. When the Bible repeats that Isaac is the son of Abraham this alludes to the fact that Isaac contained both the essence of Chesed and Gevurah, which the Zohar says is north and south or fire and water.

The integration of Chesed and Gevurah is Tiferet—an aspect of the Central Column. Jacob is Tiferet, and by his presence he brought the aspect of Central Column into this world. It therefore follows that there are three complete Sefirot in this family—Abraham (Chesed), Isaac (Gevurah), Jacob (Tiferet). The Zohar explains, however, that before Jacob came into this world, Tiferet needed to manifest itself so that Isaac's energy could be balanced and not in conflict. The Zohar says that when Isaac married Rebecca, his attained Malchut and his power—Gevurah—became manifested physically in this world. In expressing Isaac's age when he married Rebecca, the Bible is telling us that he then contained all four Sefirot (Chesed, Gevurah, Tiferet, and Malchut), and the power of Gevurah is activated only by these four Sefirot. Each Sefira contains Ten Sefirot, and four times ten is 40.

Rebecca's Essence

The Zohar continues:

> Why are we told, "The daughter of Betuel the Aramian of Paddan-aram, the sister to Laban the Arammian?" Why should we care to know all this as it had already been written, "And Betu'el sired Rivka," (Bereseheet 22:23) and now she is described as of Paddan-aram, the sister to Laban the Arammian. HE ANSWERS THAT IT IS to teach us that ALTHOUGH she was born among the misled, she did not follow their ways. Therefore it is written that she was the daughter of Betuel, of Paddan-aram, and the sister of Laban, who were all wicked and evildoers; but she did good deeds and did not behave as they did.
>
> Now we should study this further. If Rivka was twenty years old or at least thirteen, it would be considered praiseworthy that she did not do as they did. But since she was only three years old, how can she be praised for her actions? Rav Yehuda replied that although she was only three years old, she can be judged by how she behaved toward the servant. This must mean that she had the wisdom of a twenty year old, and therefore she may be praised for not learning from what they did.
> —Zohar, Toldot 2:16-17

The Zohar indicates to us that although Rebecca was born into such a negative environment, she was not influenced by her father or her brother. This is the reason we are being told who her father and brother were. Moreover, even though she was only three years old when she met Eliezer, Abraham's servant, she had the mind of a 20 year old.

Rav Yitzchak said, "Though she acted WISELY TOWARD THE SERVANT, I do not yet know if her behavior was right or not. Come and behold, it is written, 'Like the rose among thorns, so is my love among the daughters." (Shir haShirim 2:2) The rose is the congregation of Israel, NAMELY, THE NUKVA OF ZEIR ANPIN, which is among the legions as a rose among the thorns. The hidden meaning is that Isaac came from the side of Abraham, Supernal Chesed, who is kind to all creatures. And although he represented Harsh Judgment, HE NEVERTHELESS DRAWS CHESED FROM ABRAHAM. Rivka also came from the side of Harsh Judgment OF BETUEL AND LABAN. Although she was herself of Soft Judgment, IN THE SECRET OF THE REDNESS OF THE ROSE, and a thread of Chesed was attached to her, IN THE SECRET OF THE WHITENESS OF THE ROSE, nevertheless she came from Harsh Judgment. Thus, because Isaac was severe in his Judgment and Rivka was softer in her Judgment, she was "as a rose among the thorns." AND IF THE NUKVA were not of Weak Judgment, the world would not have been able to bear the Harsh Judgment of Isaac. In this manner, the Holy One, blessed be He, joins couples in the world, the harsh with the soft. THUS ISAAC WAS OF HARSH JUDGMENT AND RIVKA OF SOFT JUDGMENT, so as to balance everything. THEY WOULD BE ABLE TO RECEIVE THE LIGHT OF CHOCHMAH, and the world would be sweetened.
—Zohar, Toldot 2:18

The Zohar also explains that because Isaac was born from Abraham, who is Chesed, Isaac's harsh judgment (Gevurah) was tempered. In the same way, Rebecca's soft judgment was strengthened by her environment, so that she was on an equal footing with Isaac. This constituted a balanced soulmate relationship between them. All these aspects are what created the synchronicity between Rebecca and Isaac and what made her into his wife.

21 And Isaac prayed to the Lord on behalf of his wife, because she was barren. The Lord answered his prayer, and his wife Rebecca became pregnant.

God Desires the Prayers of the Righteous

The Zohar says there are three things that are dependent on *mazal*, which is a fixed flow of energy: number of children, years of life, and quantity of livelihood. In other words, if there will be children and how many is determined by a fixed flow of energy. How long a person lives is dependent on their DNA—a fixed flow of energy that a person receives and determines how long he or she will live. Dying a quiet death or not is not dependent on *mazal*. *Mazal* refers to when the illness or accident will overtake the person and cause death; it is the result of the energy that comes into the person. A person, during their lifetime, can influence the *mazal*. Our spiritual DNA is what determines how long we are going to live, and whether we lengthen or shorten our life.

Rebecca was barren and did not possess a reproductive system. When she was 23 years old and Isaac was 60, he prayed for her and she became pregnant. From the Bible it seems that, through his prayers, Isaac helped Rebecca to become pregnant. The Zohar explains this was not achieved merely through his prayers but rather by what the prayers contained.

One of the methods whereby the codes of the Bible may be understood is through the interchange of Hebrew letters within a word. In this case, the *Ayin* is interchanged for a *Chet* in the word *veyitar* (ויעתר to ויחתר). The Zohar says the word *veyitar* means "and he prayed." When we replace the letter *Ayin* with the letter

Chet, the word becomes *veyichtar* or "and he sought change." Through his prayer, he created a whole female system in Rebecca.

The Zohar says that they were together for 20 years and she did not conceive until he uttered this prayer. Why did it happen this way? Why did he not pray before? Why did he wait until now? Rebecca was destined to give birth regardless of the prayers of her husband. She was his soulmate, and Jacob was to be born of Isaac and Rebecca. So the Zohar asks, "Why were prayers needed?" The Zohar then answers that it happened in this way because God desires the prayers of the righteous; the Light waits for them to ask through prayer. Why is this? Both Isaac and Rebecca were righteous, therefore her reproductive organs would have appeared whether Isaac prayed or not. A righteous person can perform miracles, so why was all this necessary? The reason she was barren was because God wants the prayers of the righteous. Righteous people do not have to pray; their righteousness already makes the events occur. It was not necessary to create such a miracle through Isaac's prayer.

When the righteous pray, their prayers make a precedent in the cosmos, so that every person in a similar situation will be helped. Isaac's prayer, that a female reproductive system be created, was for all women incapable of childbearing. When a righteous person prays, they open up a channel, and when that channel is open, the flow of energy and the power of miracles is established—in this case, healing barren women. Even women who have no possibility to conceive can receive the opportunity through the merit of the prayers of the righteous. This is because the whole atmosphere changes—everything becomes one. Therefore it is written, "God answered his prayer." Isaac's prayer was not for Rebecca, it was for the entire world—the righteous have no need to pray for themselves. What is going to happen is going to happen. Isaac knew that, when the time came for Rebecca to conceive Jacob, her reproductive organs would appear. The Zohar says that even for those women who do not merit having children, everything can change by the reading of this portion on Shabbat.

Isaac understood that it was Rebecca's nature that had to be altered. He prayed because he wanted to change the complete nature of things. The Zohar says that Isaac knew, through Divine Inspiration, that the 12 tribes would come from him. He prayed because of what he knew through Divine Inspiration, and that he could and would father children. However, he was not sure if he would have children from Rebecca or through a different woman. Therefore he prayed "on behalf of his wife." It does not say that he prayed "for Rebecca." He would not pray that nature be changed by his own merit because he could not change it, although he was a righteous person.

It seems as if the Zohar contradicts what it states previously in explaining the reason that Isaac prayed. He knew that twelve tribes would descend from him, so why did he need to pray at all? Isaac prayed because he feared that something would happen and his child would intentionally commit a sin (when Jacob came to Isaac disguised as his brother Esau). Isaac's prayer extended to the world of the future, before Jacob was even born. He was praying that whatever Jacob would do in the future not be considered a disruption of the normal flow of energy, which would have upset the course of the twelve tribes. Here we see that prayer can move into and assist the future.

The Power of Miracles

Everything operates on the basis of our consciousness. Concerning the portion of Toldot, the Zohar explains that Rebecca was barren—that she had a reproductive system but could not conceive—Rebecca did not have the entire reproductive system.

By this the Zohar is telling us that a physical change occurred. Rebecca's conception was not an illusion. In fact, some have even described this conception as an immaculate conception. And for many years people altered this information about Rebecca's missing reproductive organs so that people would not become misinformed and believe that a woman without reproductive organs can conceive, as Rebecca did.

Although this event is what we refer to as a miracle, it was not for Isaac. He was a powerful channel to connect to the immaterial, metaphysical forces that are waiting to be tapped. This is what Isaac did when he prayed. What made his connection accepted by God? God is all-merciful, all-sharing, all-positive, and so this verse makes it clear that, from the point of view of the Bible, the ability to connect to miracles lies within us—in our consciousness.

The Soul, DNA, and Mind Over Matter

Our soul is the originator of our DNA. Hair color, eye color, and everything that will ever emerge in the future is already present in the DNA. Yet this knowledge was only discovered in the 20th century. Abraham, as well as Rav Shimon, the renowned kabbalist and author of the Zohar, knew that the soul is the originator of the DNA. What is the genesis of the DNA? Every person is born with their own genetic code, and every soul is complete without lack and without negativity. Through various incarnations, and as a result of our negative behavior, we pollute our soul with negativity, which, in turn, infiltrates the DNA, and along the way, things in our lives break down because this is a carry-over of our soul.

The Bible tells us we can correct our soul—we can go back to correct the origin of our suffering. In this way, Rebecca corrected whatever had to be corrected, and consequently everything was restored to a natural state, so she was able to give birth. Rebecca became pregnant because she and Isaac exercised mind over matter.

We are at a point too, where we can apply mind over matter. By instilling in our consciousness that we are able to go back and correct what needs to be corrected when chaos appears. I am not saying that if a person is ill they should not be treated by a doctor—on the physical level everything possible must be done. However, when we come up against a wall and cannot change the physical realm on the physical level, where do we go? We can go back to that place in time where we caused a defect, a break, an opportunity for Satan to enter and see if we can straighten things out. Any problem we have at present can be eliminated with *teshuvah*, which means we return to the *Hei* or go back in time remembering when our behavior was negative. Please keep in mind this does not rule out our relationship to, and effort on, the physical realm.

All that remained for Rebecca to do was on a metaphysical level. She went back and corrected what had to be repaired and therefore her DNA emerged transformed. When there is a critical mass of this consciousness, we will be able to restore ourselves physically. However, we must remember that we have to deal with the physical reality as well because the problems we encounter today, minor or major, are a result of a negative physical action from our past. Achieving the reality where mind controls matter requires reaching a certain level of consciousness, and it is important to be very careful to keep the two separate. However, this is the level we aspire to reach. The Bible readings on Shabbat help us to build up the ability to go back in time. We all encounter chaos in our lives, and when we do, there is a way to go back to before there was a problem and correct the cause of the chaos.

Praying for Miracles

Within the portion of Toldot we find the essence of what Rav Shimon knew—the capacity to create miracles is how things should be. It is a birthright. Almost 400 years ago, Rav Avraham Azulai (1570 – 1643) said that miracles will soon become a daily occurrence, and it will not take hundreds of years to get there.

The point is to move away from our old habits, our old traditions. We have not yet learned this, let alone achieved it. This is because humankind has a strong tendency to forget, while the pain and suffering of misfortune lingers. Kabbalah does provide us with the methodology for regaining memory. There is a meditation that can be performed before we pray; I am never without it. There is a structure in the universe, even though we cannot see it. Every morning, I watch the sunrise and say to myself, "The sun is shining on schedule; it is up there on time. There is order somewhere." Unfortunately, the order in the Heavens is difficult to locate down here.

The kabbalistic tools have been prepared for us, and these tools are in our possession. I always tell people to open up the Zohar and start scanning. Do we take advantage of the Ana Beko'ach, and the two Hebrew letters that govern each month? The capability of creating miracles, which was infused into the universe, is not being utilized because we do not realize that we can create miracles. We forget there is a force that we can use to improve our lives. We have all experienced miracles but perhaps we do not want to attribute them as an unusual event. Rav Abraham Azulai said Kabbalah should be made available in the marketplace.

The portion of Toldot is followed by Rosh Chodesh Kislev (New Moon of Sagittarius) and preceded by the portion of Chayei Sarah, indicating that there are conditions to creating miracles. The Bible states that God answered Isaac's prayer. What are we to understand from this statement? Are we to think that Rebecca did not pray? We must remember that Rebecca was a matriarch, so she could bear a child with her energy.

God leaned toward Isaac's prayer, and the commentators discuss this. Rashi explains that Isaac merited these benefits because his father was Abraham, whereas who was Rebecca's father? Does Rashi mean that our prayers will be answered according to who our father is? Rashi is the most concise and difficult commentator on the Bible. What we learn from this section is the importance of both praying for someone else when they need support, and of having someone else pray for us.

The Desire to Receive is strong and it runs contradictory to that of the Lightforce of God, which is to share. Rashi explains that all four sides of Abraham's tent were open so that passersby would come in. He possessed the sharing aspect and therefore had an affinity with the Lightforce. When someone, who was under the influence of the Desire to Receive needed a miracle they could come to him to receive that miracle. However, there is a fundamental rule: An aspect of sharing must accompany receiving. To breathe in we must also breathe out. To receive we must also give. This is unquestionably the technology of how to achieve miracles and draw down the Lightforce of God. It is not that God does not want to help us. When we need a miracle, when we ask for something from the Creator in our prayers simply because we need it and have no intention to share it, there is a dichotomy between us and the Lightforce of God.

This is the technology of how God operates—the energy of miracles comes with this level of technology. Although we may not want to breathe out because then we have to give, we do not question why we cannot just breathe in, we simply proceed. If I have a toothache, should I just take a painkiller? When fast temporary relief is not the objective, the rule is to ask for more because it is cleansing. There are simple techniques in every communication system. We do not stop and think about the simplest things in life—we assume that if it is too simple it cannot be true.

22 The children struggled together within her, and she said, "If it be so, why am I thus?" So she went to inquire of the Lord. 23 And the Lord said to her, "Two nations are in your womb, and two manner of people will be separated from within you; and one people will be stronger than the other people, and the older will serve the younger." 24 When the time came for her to give birth, there were twins in her womb. 25 The first came out red all over like a hairy garment; so they named him Esau. 26 And after that, his brother came out, with his hand grasping Esau's heel; and he was named Jacob. And Isaac was sixty years old when Rebecca gave birth to them.

Esau and Jacob: Two Opposing Forces

The Zohar says that Esau encapsulated all that related to Satan. Satan paints a whole picture convincing us to do things. He creates conditions by which we do things that we later realize were a mistake. Yet we are not necessarily unwise. The truth of the matter is we are being fooled by his falsehood. Once we are fooled, Satan gets us to conduct ourselves the way he wants, which brings about chaos, in whatever form it appears. Satan persuades us, he envelops us with deceit, giving us the feeling that what we see is the true picture. This is what Esau is about. In the womb, Jacob was combatting the effectiveness of Satan, preventing Satan's illusion from weaving its way around us. These two forces—positive and negative—were fighting about what the future would be at its very source.

The only way to combat the effectiveness of Satan is by creating illusions at the same time. What is being established in this section is the understanding that, when dealing with Satan, it is necessary to go with falsehood. Fight fire with fire. The Zohar is saying that the only way we can remove deceitfulness is by being deceitful. But how do we know when it is Satan? How could Jacob separate himself from Esau?

Both the Talmud and the Zohar say, "When someone is about to kill you, rise up early to kill him first." If, God forbid, someone comes with the intention of killing you, there is no question that you may kill him first.

Esau came first, and then his brother emerged with his hand holding onto Esau's heel. The Bible says, "…and He called his name Jacob." It was neither Rebecca nor Isaac who gave Jacob his name. God called him Jacob because he was holding onto the heel of Esau. Yaakov יעקב and *ekev* עקב (heel) are made up of the same letters: *Yud, Ayin, Kuf, Bet.* The Zohar says that Jacob wanted to be separated. He did not want the Snake or Satan to have influence over him, and by holding onto the heel, Jacob separated Esau from Holiness. In other words, the so-called Achilles heel, the tendon, is the place where the negativity energy becomes manifest. This is the meaning of the verse: "his hand held the heel of Esau." Jacob held onto Esau's heel the whole day and in this way the power of Holiness became dominant over Esau. Through Jacob's action, the power of Holiness, the power of positivity had dominion over negativity. This is the struggle that took place within Rebecca's womb.

Another interpretation is that Jacob's hand remained holding the heel, teaching us that we never become fully separated from the evil inclination. Jacob could not become separated totally from the Satan, therefore he later took away the Blessing of the Firstborn from Esau. Although he was born to Isaac and Rebecca, there was still a part of him that was tied to Satan. Satan is wiser than most, if not all, of us. Jacob, however, came to the world as the antithesis of the snake. The power of Jacob is that he was able to overcome the heel of Esau and that we can separate Satan from Holiness. When we connect with this reading on Shabbat, with the help of Jacob's energy, we hope to draw the energy and strength to defeat Satan. Even though he is so smart and can cloud our vision, we can take the appropriate action to fool him.

The True Nature of Prayer

In this section, the birth of two nations comes about—the two sides that humankind has been faced with ever since the Tree of Knowledge Good and Evil incident in the Garden of Eden. As mentioned previously, the portion of Toldot always appears during the month of Sagittarius (Kislev), a time of miracles. It is a gift that was given to humanity inasmuch as the Lightforce of God had known in advance that man would sin and would be subject to chaos.

We think miracles happen because God is being kind to us. Although, if we examine history, it does not require much imagination on our part to see that God does not give us many miracles. Yet we continue to pray to God, hoping for a miracle. In times of trouble, we ask God, "Where were You when I needed You most?" This does not work. It is not a question of praying to God for help. There is no such thing as prayer. God has given us such opportunities, and yet it is we who turn a deaf ear. It is amazing the good things we do not hear. The reason we do not hear is found in this portion, which details the birth of Esau, who is constantly here with us. It is that other voice within that tells us not to change: *It's only this one time; eat that piece of cake; I will start to do it tomorrow.*

How many times have we expressed rationalizations of this nature? We do not change.

The Kabbalah Centre is known as a place where transformation takes place. Does this mean we are becoming more spiritual, more sharing, more giving—in short, becoming better people? Transformation occurs when there is a change in our consciousness, a change that allows us to learn how to accept and understand the good that is in our lives and the good that is coming. The trouble is that good often seems improbable. How do we arrive at a condition of chaos? We do the wrong thing, we get the wrong information, and thus we are prone to error and are vulnerable to chaos. At the Kabbalah Centres we attempt to strengthen our consciousness so we can come to understand that transformation is for our benefit; it is not in service to God. It is how to connect, and that is to what the word "prayer" really refers.

This portion tells us how to connect with miracles. Moses orchestrated the sections of the Bible, and Toldot always occurs in the month of Sagittarius. The establishment of these connections was very precise. They are channels of energy, and we have come to extricate them from concealment that has been their lot for thousands of years. Yet still we have to battle against those who say we should be ashamed of teaching Kabbalah. By teaching Kabbalah, I want to take away chaos. If Kabbalah is watered down, it will, of course, be less effective.

Children and Change

We need miracles, yet they will not happen unless we make a conscious effort to connect to the idea that things can change. There is nothing of a chaotic nature that cannot be transformed. I know this sounds like preaching, and that what I am saying is difficult to accept. Even if it sounds right to us that is still not enough. There are forces of Esau (chaos) out there, whether they appear in the form of a human being or not. This energy force is what the Bible is referring to. Just because Esau disappeared from the scene does not mean that what he represents—negative energy—is gone.

This section conveys another beautiful idea from the Zohar. We have an opportunity, if we have a need of miracles, to use the kabbalistic tools. However, we have to place in our consciousness the fact that the moment we walk out of the Kabbalah Centre there is a good possibility we may forget what we learned and that the next day or the day after, this understanding will be completely out of our minds. This is because it is a constant war. When we come to the awareness that we are at war, then this section of Toldot—where the brothers were fighting inside Rebecca's womb—can be understood.

Rebecca wanted to find out why there was a battle inside her, and she went to seek God. The Zohar says she went to Shem and Ever's house of learning, the place where Isaac and Jacob studied. She was told by the sages that there were two nations battling in her womb, and that the first nation would be Esau and the second nation would be Jacob. With this, the Bible is telling us that the battle does not begin at age 14 or 15 but while one is but a little child.

The Zohar explains the idea of not sharing is symbolized by a child. Children have this nature inherently and need to be constantly reminded while they are maturing that there is a force of greed that thinks only for "me" and does not consider anyone else. Selfishness is the normal nature of little children. The Zohar says Satan has an open field until a child reaches the age of 13 in a male and 12 in a female.

Even a little fighting during pregnancy can be detrimental to a child's wellbeing. I suggest to couples that they take a break from arguing for at least the nine months of pregnancy. Can the chaotic inclination of humanity be changed? Yes, it begins at the very root. Even though the Zohar says that negativity is the normal tendency of children before the age of 12 and 13, it can be changed. There is nothing that cannot be changed, no matter what scientists or economists might say. Without this constant awareness in our mind 24 hours a day, we become vulnerable and make an opening for Satan. This portion is here to give the strength not normally in our possession. The fact that things can be changed must be considered every moment of the day to avoid being bombarded by other people's chaos.

27 And the boys grew, and Esau became a skillful hunter, a man of the field, and Jacob was a wholehearted person, staying among the tents. 28 And Isaac loved Esau because he ate of his venison, but Rebecca loved Jacob. 29 And Jacob was cooking soup when Esau came in from the field, famished. 30 And Esau said to Jacob, "Feed me, I pray you, with that red soup for I am famished; that is why he was also called Edom. 31 And Jacob replied, "Sell me this day your birthright." 32 And Esau said, "Look, I am about to die, what good is the birthright to me?" 33 And Jacob said, "Swear to me this day." And he swore an oath to him, and he sold his birthright to Jacob. 34 Then Jacob gave Esau some bread and some lentil soup. And he ate and drank, and then got up and left. Thus Esau despised his birthright.

Esau Sold His Birthright for Lentil Soup

Esau returned home very tired from hunting and asked Jacob to give him some food. Jacob said, "Before I give you food and satisfy your needs—namely the need of physicality—I want you to transfer to me the power of the firstborn." To surrender his energy, Esau had to replace it with something—food, money.

The teaching contained in this story is that there is a price; here energy was traded for lentil soup. On one hand, we will sell all of our energy for a trifle and Satan helps us to validate our choices. And on the other hand, we do not understand the importance of giving charity and what we receive in return, and we are also able to validate the choice of not giving. We do not understand there is always a trade-off. When we want physicality, we give something up. I am not saying that we should give all of our wealth away. How easily we are prepared to surrender energy while we are so eager to hang onto physicality.

The Nature of Time

How did Esau sell his birthright? We are certain that it is possible to go back in time—to a state before the present. The *Yud, Kaf, Shin* (ש.כ.י) letter combination from the third sentence of the Ana Beko'ach helps us to go back to the embryonic state before illnesses and chaos overtook us. Through the *Yud, Kaf, Shin*, we can literally extract ourselves from the present and go back to the past. Even science now theorizes that this is possible. There is no arguing with the fact that we can go back in time. Science is looking for the time travel machine, and Kabbalah provides it already. The *Yud, Kaf, Shin* is one of these tools.

Humanity interprets time travel as a miracle but in reality it is the norm. What is not normal is the idea that there is a yesterday, a today, and a tomorrow. What is normal is that there is no time, space or motion. What is idiotic is this notion of past, present, and future. This is what Rav Shimon explains, and what some scientists also believe. Time, space, and motion are the illusionary features of Satan. They are the means by which he makes humankind believe there is no way out of chaos. Chaos can be seen everywhere all day and all night—this is his illusion. The reason chaos exists is because too many have accepted the reality that chaos is true.

The Secret of the Redemption of the Firstborn

When Esau came back from the fields, the reason he was tired was because he had just murdered Nimrod. Isaac loved Esau and his blindness prevented him from seeing that Esau was a murderer. It says Esau felt as if he was about to die of hunger and begged Jacob for his lentil soup, which he bought with his birthright. How does a person sell something of a metaphysical nature? There is an expression that you can sell your soul to the devil. Jacob asked his brother to sell him his firstborn birthright. Why did Jacob not just give his own brother a spoonful of lentils? And it is difficult to imagine that Esau was prepared to sell it. This portion is one of the most interesting, inasmuch as it seems to be telling us how to be dishonest and how to sell ourselves to the devil. Within this famous story of Esau letting go of his birthright, the message is to never be satisfied with less in life. Go for everything.

Without Kabbalah, it is impossible to understand this story. Within this tale is our opportunity to beat Satan. Esau was the firstborn, and as such he was entitled to certain things. There is the practice of the Redemption of the Firstborn (*Pidyon HaBen*), in which the firstborn is removed from the power of Satan. Today, ninety percent of the world does not know about it. It is a tradition that has been kept a secret. In this practice it is not that the birthright is taken away but rather the firstborn is redeemed from the power of mortality.

Beresheet 26:1 And there was a famine in the land, besides the first famine of Abraham's time. And Isaac went to Abimelech, king of the Philistines in Gerar. 2 And the Lord appeared to Isaac and said, "Do not go down to Egypt; live in the land which I tell you of. 3 Stay in this land for a while, and I will be with you and will bless you. For to you and your descendants I will give all these lands and will confirm the oath I swore to Abraham, your father. 4 And I will make your seed multiply as the stars in the heaven, and will give to your seed all these countries, and in your seed all nations of the earth will be blessed, 5 because Abraham obeyed My voice and kept My charge, My commandments, My statutes, and My laws." 6 And Isaac dwelt in Gerar. 7 And the men of the place asked him about his wife, and he said, "She is my sister," because he was afraid to say, "She is my wife." He thought, "Lest the men of the place kill me for Rebecca, because she is fair to look at." 8 And it came to pass, when he had been there a long time, Abimelech, king of the Philistines, looked out of a window and saw Isaac caressing Rebecca, his wife. 9 And Abimelech called Isaac and said, "See, for sure she is your wife: and why did you say, 'She is my sister'?" And Isaac said to him, "Because I said, lest I die for her." 10 And Abimelech said, "What is this you have done to us? One of the men might well have lain with your wife, and you would have brought guilt upon us." 11 And Abimelech charged all his people, saying: "He that touches this man or his wife shall surely be put to death." 12 Then Isaac planted crops in that land and in the same year reaped a hundredfold, because the Lord blessed him. 13 And the man became great, and went forward, and grew until he became very wealthy. 14 He possessed so many flocks and possessed so many herds and a large amount of servants, and the Philistines envied him. 15 For all the wells that his father's servants had dug in the time of his father Abraham, the Philistines stopped up, and filled them with earth. 16 And Abimelech said to Isaac, "Go from us; for you are mightier than us." 17 And Isaac departed from there and pitched his tent in the Valley of Gerar and settled there. 18 And Isaac reopened the wells that had been dug in the time of Abraham his father, for the Philistines had stopped up after Abraham died, and he gave them the same names by which his father had given them. 19 And Isaac's servants dug in the valley and discovered there a well of spring water. 20 And the herdsmen of Gerar quarreled with Isaac's herdsmen, saying, "The water is ours." And he named the well Esek, because they quarreled with him. 21 And they dug another well, but they quarreled over that one also; and he named it Sitnah. 22 And he moved on from there and dug another well, and no one quarreled over it, and he named it Rehoboth, saying, "For now the Lord has made room for us and we will be fruitful in the land." 23 And he went up from there to Beersheba. 24 And the Lord appeared to him that night and said, "I am the God of Abraham, your father. Do not be afraid, for I am with you; and I will bless you and will multiply your seed for My servant Abraham's sake." 25 And he built an altar there and called upon the name of the Lord, and pitched his tent there, and there Isaac's servants dug a well. 26 Then Abimelech came to him from Gerar, with Ahuzzath, one of his friends, and Phicol, the chief captain of his army. 27 And Isaac asked them, "Why have you come to me, since you hate me and have sent me away from you?" 28 And they said, "We saw clearly that the Lord was with you; and we said, 'Let there now be an oath between us—between us and you—and let's make a covenant with you, 29 that you will do us no harm, as we have not harmed you and as we have done nothing but good to you, and have sent you away in peace. You are now the blessed of the Lord.'" 30 And he made them a feast, and they ate and drank. 31 And they rose up early in the morning and swore an oath one to each other, and Isaac sent them away, and they departed from him in peace. 32 And it came to pass that same day that Isaac's servants came and told him about the well they had dug. And they said to him, "We have found water!" 33 And he called it Shebah, and the name of the city is Beersheba till this day. 34 And Esau was forty years old when he took to wife Judith, the daughter of Beeri the Hittite, and Basemath, the daughter of Elon

the Hittite, 35 which were a source of grief to Isaac and Rebecca.

The Healing Power of Water

In this section there is the story about the re-digging of wells. It said that they found a well with Living Waters (*Mayim Chaim*). Here we have the opportunity to go back to the original state of water—pure water that has the energy for healing and rejuvenation. We should meditate on rejuvenating all the water in the world.

Beresheet 27:1 And it came to pass that when Isaac was old and his eyes dim so that he could not see, he called Esau, his older son, and said to him, "My son." And he said to him, "Behold, here I am." 2 And he said, "See, I am now old, and do not know the day of my death. 3 Now then, get, I pray you, your weapons, your quiver and your bow, and go out to the field and hunt me some venison; 4 and make me savory meat, just as I love; and bring it to me so that I may eat and that my soul may bless you before I die."

Blessing of the First Born

Esau represents the embodiment of negative thought energy-intelligence—the force that entices us do the wrong thing. Jacob was the embodiment of Central Column—restriction and balance. So how could Isaac, a man who can control the forces of nature, not see the difference between Esau and Jacob? Isaac was not just a regular person, the kind we could justify making a mistake. Isaac knew exactly what he was doing when he told Esau that he wanted to give him the Blessing of the Firstborn.

In fact, the Zohar explains that Isaac was giving an eternal blessing, a transference of energy. Here, Isaac, the man for whom all the laws of nature complied, was to transfer this positive energy force to Esau. But there could never be that connection, no matter what was going to happen. If this were to take place, the Zohar states that evil would have become eternal. Did Isaac not realize that there was this possibility? The Zohar explains that things do not change, they only appear to change. There are times that, no matter what our intentions, if our consciousness is in the right place, the wrong thing will never come about. We can do the most foolhardy things and it will work out in the end. The reverse is also true, there times when all our beautiful plans wind up as a pile of mud. In Isaac's mind, Esau was the one who was destined to get that blessing because his own power could only connect with a power of similar affinity.

It might seem as though Isaac made a mistake but he did not. Everything conforms to the laws and principles of this universe. Those incidents that appear to go outside the natural laws and principles of the universe can do so because ninety-nine percent of these atoms say "I am here for the expressed purpose of serving humankind." Only humanity has this capacity. Humankind is the Malchut that controls everything around us. The only plans that come to fruition are those that are connected to the consciousness of making yesterday and tomorrow both present here and now. This all depends on where our head is at. Physical manifestation of good or evil is not good and is not evil. It is only evil if someone's head is in an evil frame of mind. Things are so relative in this world that we must come to one conclusion: everything on a physical corporeal reality level is really an illusion. At first something that seems to have turned out bad can become a blessing two days later. We cannot say something is all bad, and we cannot say it is all good. The market goes up and the market goes down. For one person, it is always a blessing, and for one, it is always a curse. Is the market bad for everybody when it goes down? Is the market good for everyone when it goes up?

When our head is right, and we are sharing and restricting, the atoms will do the work for us. We do not need to worry about what happens because it will happen by itself. If Esau was destined to receive the blessing he would have received the blessing. Isaac was a channel for positive Left Column energy, meaning the Desire to Receive for the Sake of Sharing. He was not a channel for the Desire to Receive for Oneself Alone. Abraham was not a channel for the Desire to Receive at all; he embodied a pure sharing concept. He never asked for anyone to bring him anything, as Isaac did with Esau. Isaac was of a pure mind, therefore he would do the right thing. He was going to share his blessing, and the result of that thought would manifest itself in a positive way, even if the illusion appeared to be contrary. Maybe the road would be bumpy along the way but in the end the result would be of a positive nature, and Esau would not be evil.

When we think we have helped someone, the reality is that the other person is only there to give us an opportunity to share so that we can make a connection. Essentially we are not giving to the one we have helped because if there were no poor people around how could we share? How could we make our connection with the Lightforce, which is an internal characteristic of sharing?

The Nature of the Relationship between Isaac and Esau

When Isaac felt he was getting old and his eyes were no longer working properly, he called Esau to him because he wanted to give Esau a blessing. Esau had sold his birthright to his brother for lentil soup. We do this every day; we trade off valuable things—life, happiness, joy—for trifles.

Isaac did not know that his son Esau had sold his birthright. The blessing for the birthright indicated that he loved Esau more than Jacob. Was there such a preference for one child more than another, as there is found in most families? Is this right? No. This is absolutely wrong. Isaac represents Chesed of the Left Column, and so he also represents Receiving for the Sake of Sharing, while Esau represents Gevurah of Left Column, Receiving for the Self Alone.

They share a common denominator—Desire to Receive—and this is why Isaac sought to give the blessing to Esau.

5 And Rebecca heard when Isaac spoke to his son Esau. And Esau went to the field to hunt for venison and bring it back. 6 And Rebecca said to her son Jacob, "Look, I heard your father say to Esau, your brother, 7 'Bring me venison and make me savory meat that I may eat, and bless you before the Lord, before my death.' 8 Now, therefore, my son, obey my voice and do what I command you: 9 Go now to the flock and fetch me from there two choice kid goats, and I will make from them savory meat for your father, just the way he loves it. 10 And you will take it to your father so that he may eat, and that he may bless you before his death." 11 And Jacob said to Rebecca his mother, "But Esau, my brother is a hairy man, and I am a man with smooth skin. 12 What if my father will touch me and I would appear to be deceiving him? I will bring a curse upon myself and not a blessing." 13 And his mother said to him, "Let the curse fall on me, my son. Just obey my voice and go fetch them for me." 14 And he went and fetched, and brought them to his mother, and his mother made savory meat, just the way his father loved it. 15 And Rebecca took the best clothes of her older son, Esau, which were in her house, and put them on Jacob, her younger son; 16 and she put the skins of kid goats over his hands and upon the smooth part of his neck; 17 and she gave the savory meat and bread which she had prepared into the hand of her son Jacob. 18 And he came to his father and

said, "My father." And he said, "Here I am. Who are you, my son?" 19 And Jacob said to his father, "I am Esau, your firstborn. I have done as you have told me. I pray you, sit and eat of my venison that your soul may bless me." 20 And Isaac said to his son, "How is it that you have found it so quickly, my son?" And he said, "The Lord your God brought it to me." 21 And Isaac said to Jacob, "Come near, I pray you, that I may feel you, my son, to know whether you really are my son Esau or not." 22 And Jacob went near to Isaac, his father, and he felt him and said, "The voice is the voice of Jacob, but the hands are the hands of Esau." 23 And he did not recognize him, because his hands were hairy like those of his brother Esau's; so he blessed him. 24 And he said, "Are you really my son Esau?" And he said, "I am." 25 And he said, "Bring it near to me and I will eat my son's venison, that my soul may bless you." And he brought it near to him and he ate; and he brought him wine and he drank. 26 And his father Isaac said to him, "Come near now, and kiss me, my son." 27 And he came near and kissed him, and he smelled the smell of his clothes, and blessed him and said, "See, the smell of my son is the smell of a field which the Lord has blessed: 28 Therefore God give you of the dew of heaven, and the fatness of the earth, and plenty of grain and wine; 29 let people serve you and nations bow down to you. Be lord over your brethren, and let your mother's sons bow down to you: May those

who curse you be cursed and those who bless you be blessed."

Isaac as a Chariot

When Isaac said to Jacob, "Who are you my son?" Jacob answered, "I am your firstborn Esau, and I've done what you asked. I brought back venison, now bless me." Isaac asked Jacob to draw close because he wanted to make sure that it was Esau. Jacob drew close, and Isaac said "the voice is of Jacob and the hands are those of Esau." He did not recognize Jacob, and therefore he blessed him.

Isaac kissed his son and blessed him, giving him everything of a material, as well as an immaterial, nature. Isaac and Jacob are patriarchs, and prophets. They are chariots who are connected to the Upper World where there is no time, space, and motion, and they have complete control over the physical world. The reason the kabbalists use the word "chariot" is because it is like the saddle on a horse that connects the horse with its rider. They connect the physical world with the upper, metaphysical, world. They are people of inestimable caliber and consciousness.

Jacob Took the Blessing

Jacob lied to his father, saying he was his firstborn son. How could Jacob the chariot, who lived in the reality of the Tree of Life, lie? The commentators struggled with this concept and translated his answer to be: "I am who I am." The Zohar helps us to understand the deeper ideas, for what is here is a coded message. Esau murdered Nimrod and stole Adam's cloak, which was in Nimrod's possession. Adam's cloak attracted animals immediately to whoever was wearing it. When Esau wore that cloak, animals would bow down to him, making it easy for him to hunt them. Rebecca told Jacob to put on the cloak so he would be able to hunt and slaughter the animal for his father. Was this the nature of the deception of the matriarchs and patriarchs? This story represents the opening to connect with blessings, now and whenever we might find ourselves in despair. We have the opportunity with connections—I do not call them prayers—to tap into the awesome energy and miracles necessary to remove chaos from our lives.

Did Isaac Truly Not Recognize Jacob?

Isaac asked Jacob how it was that he returned so quickly, and Jacob responded (as Esau), saying that God was with him. How was it that all of a sudden his son Esau was speaking about God? Isaac had never heard Esau speak this way before.

Isaac asked his son to come closer so that he could touch him to see if he was really Esau. Does this not strike you as odd? Isaac touched him and said, "Your voice sounds like Jacob but when I touch your hands they are like Esau." Despite these misgivings, Isaac blessed him. And then he asked him again, "Are you my son?" Although the Bible states that his eyes grew dim, Isaac was of course aware. This is the Holy Bible, our manual of how to improve our lives. What is this conversation about? What does this all mean? Jacob responded affirmatively, and Isaac gave him all the blessings, which constituted the entirety of the Tree of Life—the Flawless Universe. Who does not want the Flawless Universe? Jacob came with deceit to receive the blessing. By what right did he come to get the blessing from his father? Is the lesson here that a lie is permitted? This is not even a white lie. In verse 24 it says, "Are you my son Esau?" And Jacob answered, "*Ani*" or "I am." The word *ani* (אני) is one of the 72 Names of God. When Jacob came close to Isaac, Isaac smelled Jacob's clothing—the coat of Adam had the scent of the Garden of

Eden. The Zohar gives us the clear explanation: Humankind has to play this game of life correctly, and Kabbalah gives us the tools to do so.

It is commonly assumed that Jacob's taking of the blessing from Isaac was a deception, since Isaac wanted to give the blessing to Esau. However, this kind of deception is not what the Bible is talking about. The story is only a clue as to how to deceive Satan. For example, when we immerse ourselves in the *mikveh* (ritual bath to cleanse ourselves spiritually), we meditate on the Hebrew letters of *Yud, Kaf, Shin* from the Ana Beko'ach. With the *Yud, Kaf, Shin* we are fooling the Satan by withdrawing the life-force that he feeds on. In the case of the disease of cancer, the difficulty is that Satan is eating away and multiplying. We are totally indebted to the Zohar for giving us this technology. The *Yud, Kaf, Shin* takes the life-force from the cell and for only an instant the cell dies; although it does not really die. The second that the cell dies, the Satan leaves. Without a living source of nourishment, Satan has no reason to stay.

The Desire to Receive is never fulfilled. This is the nature of Satan. The *Yud, Kaf, Shin* removes the Lightforce, which is Satan's nourishment, and then afterwards restores it once again. When the Satan is no longer present, the *Yud, Kaf, Shin* restores the cellular life-force. In effect, through this deception we make Satan believe that the cell is dead. This is what the Bible is teaching us through the story of the deception of Esau by Jacob.

By the reading of the portion we receive the strength to do the same—to deceive Satan through transformation—to convert what is negative into something positive. When talking about the negative entities in our body, there is no lasting blessing from cutting out negativity. We cannot destroy disease with a magic bullet. There is no instant pill. We need the filament. We need to act through the power of restriction, to behave differently, to convert that which is negative within to remove the chaos from ourselves.

The lesson we learn here is that there is no enemy outside of ourselves. One cannot eliminate negativity by removing a dictator or a cancer cell. Every dictator is replaced by another, and cancer often remains uncured. We forget that there is nothing new. As long as we do not transform ourselves, the negativity will remain.

We Are All Involved With Chaos

Esau discovered how his blessing was lost and he wept, saying that he is going to kill his brother Jacob. Why would he do this when he had already knowingly sold his birthright to Jacob? Such is the nature of life: We always look upon our misfortunes in terms of "buts" and "ifs." We are all involved with chaos in one form or another. The chaos that might trump us tomorrow is a mystery to all of us, and that is why we come to connect with the Torah reading on Shabbat.

30 And it came to pass as soon as Isaac finished blessing Jacob and Jacob had scarcely left the presence of Isaac his father, that Esau, his brother, came in from his hunting. 31 And he also had made savory meat, and brought it to his father, and said to father, "Let my father arise and eat of his son's venison, that your soul may bless me." 32 And Isaac, his father said to him, "Who are you?" And he said, "I am your son, your firstborn, Esau." 33 And Isaac trembled violently and said, "Who and where is he that took venison and brought it to me, and I have eaten it all before you came and have blessed him? Yes, and he will be blessed." 34 When Esau heard his father's words, he burst out with a loud and bitter cry and said to his father, "Bless me also, O my father" 35 And he said, "Your brother came deceitfully and took away your blessing." 36 And he said, "Isn't he rightly named Jacob? He has deceived me these two times: He took away my birthright, and now he has taken away my blessing!" And he said, "Have you not reserved any blessing for me?" 37 And Isaac answered and said to Esau, "See, I have made him lord over you and have made all his brethren his servants, and I have sustained him with grain and wine. So what can I possibly do for you now, my son?" 38 And Esau said to his father, "Do you have only one blessing, my father? Bless me too, O my father." And Esau raised his voice and wept. 39 And Isaac, his father, answered him, "Behold, your dwelling will be away from

the earth's richness, away from the dew of heaven above. 40 You will live by the sword and you will serve your brother. But when you grow restless, you will throw his yoke from off your neck."

We Also Trade Energy for Lentil Soup

After Jacob received the blessing, Esau came to bring his father the venison as he requested, and a shudder overcame Isaac as he said the same words, "Who are you? I already blessed the one who brought me food." Esau cried with bitterness, and asked why he, too, could not be blessed. This illustrates how Satan functions; he builds up a process, a case for confusion. Esau saw that his brother deceitfully took his blessing. The younger brother was called Jacob because he could manipulate things. He also realized that this was the second time Jacob had fooled him—the first time was when he took his birthright—and now Jacob had stolen his blessing. Esau became wiser, as we often do after we realize what can be lost. He understood what he gave up, and he wanted to go back. Although Esau did not want to tell his father that he sold his birthright, he asked his father to bless him as well but Isaac could not give the blessing of the firstborn twice.

Three thousand people walk into the Kabbalah Centre every year, and ninety-nine percent of them believe in ninety-nine percent of what we teach. Then they trade it for lentil soup. It is like a child holding on to the ledge as the father reaches out, but the child slips away from him. I see friends as they slip away. They say, "Hold on to me, don't let me go!" As much as the father wants to hold on, the child still slips away. They slip away because they are trading the energy that they capture. We see the truth only when it is too late.

Only then do we try to go back. Esau slipped off that ledge when he sold his birthright, but Jacob was far more prudent.

Like Esau, we look for someone to blame for all the right reasons, without first looking inside. Esau was foolish enough to sell his precious birthright for something material, revealing to us the way we justify our actions. We know that energy can be traded. There is a simple Universal Law: When we utter evil speech about another person, all the positive actions of that day are transferred to them. Why should we squander all the energy we received in exchange for a moment's trivial pleasure, for the thrill of gossiping? We bring upon ourselves our problems, when we are prepared to trade our energy for a little lentil soup.

Shabbat is an example, and I am not here to suggest that one should come to Shabbat and to what extent one needs to participate. However, when I travel, I take my own Sefer Torah and ten people because, without the reading of Shabbat, we can forget having the energy to overcome the powerful force of Satan. It is impossible otherwise to avoid pitfalls of the lentil soup.

Time Travel: How Jacob Became the Firstborn

Why did Esau say that Jacob fooled him a second time? What Jacob did was with Esau's permission. If Jacob did not have Esau's permission it would have been against the natural laws of the universe, which no one can circumvent. Despite all the rationalizations we use to steal, to kill, to hurt for all the good reasons, the natural laws are inviolable. If Jacob did not have Esau's permission, he could not have taken the birthright of the firstborn for a little lentil soup. What is being discussed here is the energy of all the things that we can accomplish—just as Jacob did when

he became the firstborn. Jacob was able to do this because he
was a chariot.

Steven Spielberg's film, *Back to the Future*, illustrates the
complications and paradoxes of time travel. Is it actually possible
to go back in time? For example, say I was born to my father and
mother, but I did not think it was a good marriage, so I went back
in time and stopped the marriage. Now here's the problem with
this: if there is no marriage, there is no me. So how can I go back
in time? This is one of the great paradoxes of time travel. If you are
here, you can go back but then you are not here. Science says time
travel is fundamentally impossible because the slightest change
to the past alters the future totally—but we have to rethink this
notion. The point is that Jacob did go back in time. The important
lesson found in this biblical reading is that we can go back in time.
The *Yud, Kaf, Shin*, which is part of the Ana Beko'ach, is how
Jacob became the firstborn. Isaac knew that Jacob altered the order
of birth.

Energy and Consciousness

What the Bible is discussing here is not a blessing of Esau, it is
speaking of consciousness. If a father blesses his child yet is thinking
about the World Series, what kind of blessing does the son receive?
Our thoughts affect the physical world. Isaac knew who Esau was.
To channel all the Lightforce of God, an energy vessel is needed,
and this was Esau.

To be rid of negativity, of cancer or financial problems, the solution
cannot simply be to cut it out. The emphasis should be on letting
more Light into the darkness. When there is darkness, turn on
the Light. Conventional wisdom says that, whatever the problem
is, cut it out. But when negativity is cut out, a space is created,

and because there cannot be a vacuum in nature, any kind of void will simply be filled with another corruption. The only process by which we can convert a cancer cell into a healthy cell is to change the darkness into something good. Cutting out cancer is not the answer; the cell is a building block. The blessing given by Isaac is an infusion of the Lightforce of God. If it was Esau who received it, he would have absorbed this blessing and the energy would have been wasted. Anything that exists is a *tikkun* (spiritual correction) process. I am saying that one can transform the body to repair the cancer cell, not cut it out. If it is cut out, it will be replaced by another darkness.

Ana Beko'ach and Undoing Disorder

The Ana Beko'ach prayer has the power of letter combinations that take us back to the state of Adam before he sinned, before he chose the Tree of Knowledge of Good and Evil, when he was in the consciousness of the Tree of Life, where there is no death and no chaos.

First Line of the Ana Beko'ach: *AB"G YT"Z –* אב"ג ית"ץ
This is the letter combination that has the power to undo material consciousness and restore us to the state of Adam before the sin.

Second line of the Ana Beko'ach: *KR"A ST"N –* קר"ע שט"ן
This line forms the acronym *Kra Satan* or "tear Satan." What is Satan? After Adam ate the apple for the second time, he chose the Tree of Knowledge of Good and Evil and made room for Satan to operate. What is Satan's power? It is to confuse the letter combinations, and this causes disorder. Certain faults in people can be caused by jumbled letter combinations, and this is the confusion that Satan brings. *Kra Satan* undoes this disorder.

Satan has millions of letter combinations. Just as there is a letter combination for the word "table," so there are combinations of letters for everything in this world. An individual who can see but has evil eye has a defect in his eye because Satan changed the combination of the word "eye." Every limb has a combination and, if we know these combinations, we can divert Satan's intentions and rid ourselves of all disease. Daily we grow closer to this point of understanding. Only recently did I myself truly begin to understand what Ana Beko'ach is all about, what power there is in the first combination, *AB"G Y"TZ.*

We have been reciting Ana Beko'ach for years, and in the merit of not praying but making our connections with intent as we say *Amen*, we are narrowing the gap in understanding daily. We must therefore make our connections with consciousness. We need to *feel* prayer and direct it. How fortunate we are that new knowledge arrives every day, but this new knowledge brings more and more confusion into the world. People may not be able to understand what is happening with these changes, and they will look for a way out of it. They will search and try to understand how order may be restored.

41 And Esau hated Jacob because of the blessing his father had given him. And Esau said to himself, "The days of mourning for my father are near; then I will kill my brother Jacob." 42 And these words of Esau her oldest son, were told to Rebecca, and she sent for her younger son Jacob and said to him, "Behold, your brother Esau, as touching you, is consoling himself with the thought of killing you. 43 Now then, my son, obey my voice: Arise and flee to my brother Laban in Haran. 44 Stay with him for a few days until your brother's fury turns away, 45 until your brother's anger turns away from you and he forgets what you did to him. Then I will send and fetch you back from there. Why should I be deprived of you both in one day?"

Space is an Illusion: Jacob and Joseph

Esau said he would kill Jacob as soon as his father died. Rebecca advised Jacob that his brother wanted to kill him, and she told him to run away to her brother Laban's house and stay there until Esau's anger disappeared. Immediately following this statement by Rebecca, it says again, "Until your brother's anger turns away from you," which is redundant. Previously we discussed another repetition during the blessing of Jacob, the stress Isaac put upon asking who Jacob was, and the first response was "I am Esau," and then a few verses later, when Jacob was asked again, he replied "*ani*." Twice Isaac had to ask who he was but there was a separation of many verses between the first "Who are you?" and the second. Here, there is no separation between the repetition, it occurs immediately. Why is this? The answer is so simple, it is so deep, and it is such an important lesson that we should never forget it. Rebecca told Jacob to stay at her brother's home until Esau's anger abated. Jacob asked, "How will I know that it is lifted?" She responded, "Even though you will be a thousand miles away, you will know when this anger is lifted from you and your thoughts."

The Bible teaches us here that space is not a problem. There is the phenomenon of telepathy; people separated by time, space, and motion can nevertheless communicate. There are other names for this phenomenon, but telepathy is a fact. Here the Bible tells us there is no reason why time, space, and motion should be limiting factors in our lives. This is the purpose of this reading, and of the biblical redundancy. We do not have to be in physical contact to know what is going on everywhere. Space, as we know it, is one of those illusions that cause us chaos, and with this reading we want to get rid of that aspect of the illusion so that we are not separated by space.

46 And Rebecca said to Isaac, "I am weary of my life because of the daughters of Heth. If Jacob takes a wife from among the daughters of Heth, these daughters of the land, what good shall my life do me?"

The Letter Kuf and the Resurrection of the Dead

Rebecca said to Isaac, "I am weary of my life." The word *katzti*, "I am weary" or "had enough of" is written with a small *Kuf*. The *Kuf* is the only Hebrew letter that descends below the line. This is the letter that gives life to the world of the *klipot* (shells), to the world of Satan. We know that Satan has no energy of his own and that he only has the energy we impart to him. The body has no life-force without the soul; it could not exist on its own. Take electricity, for example, we see how electricity is actualized but we do not see electricity itself. The reason that the letter *Kuf* is reduced in size in the word *katzti* is because the letter ascended to the Upper World to bring about the end, to bring an end to the end—the Resurrection of the Dead. Death is an illusion. This is why it is written that one who does not believe in the Resurrection of the Dead is a heretic, for this is, in fact, the principle upon which everything exists.

The Finite and Chaos

The word *katzti* comes from the word *ketz*, meaning "chaos" or "finite." The definition of chaos is the consciousness of finite. It is the mental process that causes us to believe there must be an end. This is the cause of all problems in the world.

The *Kuf* is small in the word *katzti*, so that the letter does not go below the line. The *Kuf* is the only letter that goes below the line, as opposed to the letter *Lamed*, which goes above the line. And because it is small, the energy source of chaos can be removed. Through this section we would like to remove every aspect of the finite, which is mortality, from our consciousness, thereby removing the cause of all chaos in our lives.

Understanding the Kuf

There is nothing as powerful as the small letter *Kuf*, but first we have to understand what the *Kuf* is. The Zohar explains that the reason we call this letter *Kuf* is because it also means "monkey." Rav Isaac Luria (the Ari 1534 – 1572), said 400 years ago that there will come a time when science will think that humans came from monkeys. Medical science today does all of the cancer research on monkeys since they are the closest creatures we have to humans; the only difference is the opposable thumb. *Kuf* represents the monkey, which is like a human—only it is an animal with five fingers except for the difference in the thumbs.

We have to understand that Satan cannot operate without fuel, without being instilled with sparks of Light. Humans have the smallest degree of the Lightforce but still we are higher than other lifeforms. Energy means there is movement—there are atoms moving around, everything must contain the Lightforce. The Zohar says the *Kuf* acts as the vehicle that supplies all of the corrupt sequences in our bodies with Light and energy. For most of us, it was inconceivable only 50 years ago that a man would walk on the moon.

With Kabbalah we want to see what is happening before we slip away—like the child off the ledge. Once we have created a short circuit, we want to go back, and when we realize we cannot, we get angry and violent. The small *Kuf* in the word *ketz*, which the

English translation says means "weary," actually means "end or finite." This is the reason why time is an illusion. It is we who have the benefit to try to raise consciousness. I even once read in the New York Times that time is an illusion. Only Satan represents an end. Immortality does not include Satan, and the process of time is only related to Satan. We have the good fortune today to understand all of these connections, so we need to appreciate them or the energy will slip away. With the small *Kuf* we can cause Satan to slip away instead.

Beresheet 28:1 And Isaac called Jacob and blessed him and charged him, saying: "You shall not take a wife of the daughters of Canaan. 2 Arise, go to Paddan Aram, to the house of Bethuel, your mother's father, and there take a wife for yourself from the daughters of Laban, your mother's brother. 3 May God Almighty bless you, and make you fruitful and multiply you that you may become a multitude of people. 4 And give the blessing of Abraham to you and your seed with you, so that you may inherit the land where you are now a stranger, the land which God gave to Abraham." 5 And Isaac sent Jacob away, and he went to Paddan Aram, to Laban, son of Bethuel the Syrian, the brother of Rebecca, Jacob and Esau's mother. 6 When Esau saw that Isaac had blessed Jacob and had sent him away to Paddan Aram to take a wife from there, and that when he blessed him he charged him saying, "You shall not take a wife of the daughters of Canaan;" 7 and that Jacob obeyed his father and his mother and had gone to Paddan Aram; 8 Esau realized how displeasing the daughters of Canaan were to Isaac, his father; 9 so he went to Ishmael and married Mahalath, daughter of Ishmael, Abraham's son, the sister of Nebaioth, in addition to the wives he already had.

The Importance of Amen

After Jacob took the birthright from Esau, and Rebecca heard that Esau wanted to kill his brother, she told Jacob to go to Haran until his brother's anger abated. How could this be? If Jacob was in Haran and Esau was in Canaan, how would he know when it would be safe to come home? We know that time, space, and motion are illusionary, so Jacob *could* know because he knew how to feel. He had the ability to feel another person, to transcend time, space, and motion. This transcendence makes it possible to sense another person. It is very important to know this and to actualize this knowledge in our prayer connections.

During our prayer connections as a community, it is important for everyone to focus on each and every *Amen* that is uttered, to mentally connect Zeir Anpin and Malchut in both of their combinations. This would include the *Amen* in the *Kaddish* and the *Amen* in the blessings, and all other points in the prayers in which we answer, *Amen*. The one who answers *Amen* is even more empowered than the one who recites the blessing because answering *Amen* is more important than the entire prayer. The purpose of answering *Amen* is to elevate everything in our world, even our breath, to the consciousness of *one*, and to narrow the gap between ourselves and the Light. For this gap is none other than Satan.

Why is answering *Amen* the most important part of prayer? It says in the Talmud that when a person answers *Amen* he can attain his world; in a single minute he can unify everything. We receive more by answering *Amen* because we are the root of this process. There is so much power in being the root. All the fruits that emerge from this are returned to the one who recites *Amen*. With God's help, the distance and the time between the root and the fruit will become shorter, and we will see the fruits of The Kabbalah Centre's efforts as quickly as possible. This is the power of *Amen*: Shortening the time and the gap that is Satan.

There has been no change for thousands of years because people do not know how to pray and do not know the purpose of *Amen*. How fortunate are we to know this. For more on the power of answering *Amen*, refer to the Zohar, Volume 16, in the section of Vayelech, paragraph 36.

At the time of Creation, it was on the fourth day that the moon was diminished. As we know, the moon symbolizes Malchut, and we want to prevail upon this root and bring Malchut back to be like Zeir Anpin, like the sun—and this is what we do when we answer, *Amen*.

Who is conscious of the harm they do? The evil eye, slander, selfish desires? It is so important that there be unity in our community. It makes no difference what each person thinks; what is important is that there be unity among us. We are working for the Light, yet we get into arguments and squabble among ourselves for the sake of the Light. If you are really working for the Light, if you are with the Light, then keep quiet and let the Light work because unity is paramount. Unity is all we have left to protect the core. It is all that remains.

Two people may have different opinions and both may be right. For example, when we view the picture that includes both an image of a goblet and two faces, the optical illusion is that sometimes you can see only one image and sometimes you see that there are really two different images that are part of the same picture. Both aspects are part and correct, even though one person may see a different image than his friend.

The Afterlife

In the section of the Zohar related to this portion, there is a long examination of the World to Come. What is the "Hereafter"? Is it after here? Where is "after here" precisely? Is it that when someone dies, they go to the world after? Science does not subscribe to this interpretation. The Zohar spends a lot of ink on this discussion. Ultimately, what this means is that those who do good things in this world merit rewards in the Hereafter.

This is nothing new, but the Zohar brings a fresh interpretation. Everything mentioned in the portion of Toldot is not talking about this physical world but the afterlife. The Zohar explains that there are parallel universes, which exist right here and everywhere. There is the world we are familiar with, and then there is another world right here that, for the most part, we cannot see. It is the world where all the righteous people who have fulfilled their *tikkun* process exist. There is a thin, opaque layer over this world so that we cannot see it. Sometimes we hear it, but we do not pay attention. It is the Flawless World, without the chaos so well known to humankind.

According to the Zohar, immortality exists today, and those who pass away from this dimension go through that curtain. The person who dies is standing right next to their loved ones. Because so many of us have accepted that there is not a Hereafter, another world, a whole and different dimension, the curtain that separates us from it remains drawn. Science agrees there is another dimension with no time, space or motion, and says there are parallel universes. We know that the other world is a Flawless Universe. We say this outright and people laugh at us but we do not mind. The Zohar says Toldot is about understanding that time, space, and motion is an illusion.

Conclusion

Regarding the portion of Toldot, the Zohar speaks about Abraham and Isaac, and the issue of *Mashiach* (Messiah) and *tzadikim* (righteous people), who want to acquire the pleasure of the World to Come, which I stress is not in the Heavens. I hope that we can receive this consciousness of the World to Come, which is the consciousness of the Tree of Life that exists now for the righteous. We need to understand that to get to the World to Come, we need to become a *tzadik*—though not a *tzadik* in the sense of making decisions about right and wrong. Why do we not understand that if we do not do what is right, we will pay for it later? This is the consciousness that is too often missing, and I hope that with the merit of this portion we can reach such a level.

About the Centres

Kabbalah is the deepest and most hidden meaning of the Torah or Bible. Through the ultimate knowledge and mystical practices of Kabbalah, one can reach the highest spiritual levels attainable. Although many people rely on belief, faith, and dogmas in pursuing the meaning of life, Kabbalists seek a spiritual connection with the Creator and the forces of the Creator, so that the strange becomes familiar, and faith becomes knowledge.

Throughout history, those who knew and practiced the Kabbalah were extremely careful in their dissemination of the knowledge because they knew the masses of mankind had not yet prepared for the ultimate truth of existence. Today, kabbalists know that it is not only proper but necessary to make the Kabbalah available to all who seek it.

The Research Centre of Kabbalah is an independent, non-profit institute founded in Israel in 1922. The Centre provides research, information, and assistance to those who seek the insights of Kabbalah. The Centre offers public lectures, classes, seminars, and excursions to mystical sites at branches in Israel and in the United States. Branches have been opened in Mexico, Montreal, Toronto, Paris, Hong Kong, and Taiwan.

Our courses and materials deal with the Zoharic understanding of each weekly portion of the Torah. Every facet of life is covered and other dimensions, hithertofore unknown, provide a deeper connection to a superior reality. Three important beginner courses cover such aspects as: Time, Space and Motion; Reincarnation, Marriage, Divorce; Kabbalistic Meditation; Limitation of the Five Senses; Illusion-Reality; Four Phases; Male and Female, Death, Sleep, Dreams; Food; and Shabbat.

Thousands of people have benefited from the Centre's activities, and the Centre's publishing of kabbalistic material continues to be the most comprehensive of its kind in the world, including translations in English, Hebrew, Russian, German, Portuguese, French, Spanish, Farsi (Persian).

Kabbalah can provide one with the true meaning of their being and the knowledge necessary for their ultimate benefit. It can show one spirituality that is beyond belief. The Research Centre of Kabbalah will continue to make available the Kabbalah to all those who seek it.

— Rav Berg, 1984

About The Zohar

The Zohar, the basic source of the Kabbalah, was authored two thousand years ago by Rabbi Shimon bar Yochai while hiding from the Romans in a cave in Peki'in for 13 years. It was later brought to light by Rabbi Moses de Leon in Spain, and further revealed through the Safed Kabbalists and the Lurianic system of Kabbalah.

The programs of the Research Centre of Kabbalah have been established to provide opportunities for learning, teaching, research, and demonstration of specialized knowledge drawn from the ageless wisdom of the Zohar and the Jewish sages. Long kept from the masses, today this knowledge of the Zohar and Kabbalah should be shared by all who seek to understand the deeper meaning of this spiritual heritage, and a deeper and more profound meaning of life. Modern science is only beginning to discover what our sages veiled in symbolism. This knowledge is of a very practical nature and can be applied daily for the betterment of our lives and of humankind.

Darkness cannot prevail in the presence of Light. Even a darkened room must respond to the lighting of a candle. As we share this moment together we are beginning to witness, and indeed some of us are already participating in, a people's revolution of enlightenment. The darkened clouds of strife and conflict will make their presence felt only as long as the Eternal Light remains concealed.

The Zohar now remains an ultimate, if not the only, solution to infusing the cosmos with the revealed Lightforce of the Creator. The Zohar is not a book about religion. Rather, the Zohar is concerned with the relationship between the unseen forces of the cosmos, the Lightforce, and the impact on humanity.

The Zohar promises that with the ushering in of the Age of Aquarius, the cosmos will become readily accessible to human understanding. It states that in the days of the Messiah "there will no longer be the necessity for one to request of his neighbor, teach me wisdom." (Zohar, Naso 9:65) "One day, they will no longer teach every man his neighbor and every man his brother, saying know the Lord. For they shall all know Me, from the youngest to the oldest of them." (Jeremiah 31:34)

We can, and must, regain dominion of our lives and environment. To achieve this objective, the Zohar provides us with an opportunity to transcend the crushing weight of universal negativity.

The daily perusing of the Zohar, without any attempt at translation or understanding will fill our consciousness with the Light, improving our well-being, and influencing all in our environment toward positive attitudes. Even the scanning of the Zohar by those unfamiliar with the Hebrew *Alef Bet* will accomplish the same result.

The connection that we establish through scanning the Zohar is one of unity with the Light of the Creator. The letters, even if we do not consciously know Hebrew or Aramaic, are the channels through which the connection is made and can be likened to dialing the right telephone number or typing in the right codes to run a computer program. The connection is established at the metaphysical level of our being and radiates into our physical plane of existence. But first there is the prerequisite of metaphysical "fixing." We have to consciously, through positive thought and actions, permit the immense power of the Zohar to radiate love, harmony, and peace into our lives for us to share with all humanity and the universe.

As we enter the years ahead, the Zohar will continue to be a people's book, striking a sympathetic chord in the hearts and minds of those who long for peace, truth, and relief from suffering. In the face of crises and catastrophe, the Zohar has the ability to resolve agonizing human afflictions by restoring each individual's relationship with the Lightforce of the Creator.

— Rav Berg, 1984

Kabbalah Centre Books

72 Names of God, The: Technology for the Soul
72 Names of God for Kids, The: A Treasury of Timeless Wisdom
72 Names of God Meditation Book, The
And You Shall Choose Life: An Essay on Kabbalah, the Purpose of Life, and Our True Spiritual Work
Angel Intelligence: How Your Consciousness Determines Which Angels Come Into Your Life
AstrologiK: Kabbalistic Astrology Guide for Children
Becoming Like God: Kabbalah and Our Ultimate Destiny
Beloved of My Soul: Letters of Our Master and Teacher Rav Yehuda Tzvi Brandwein to His Beloved Student Kabbalist Rav Berg
Consciousness and the Cosmos (Previously Star Connection)
Days of Connection: A Guide to Kabbalah's Holidays and New Moons
Days of Power Part 1
Days of Power Part 2
Dialing God: Daily Connection Book
Education of a Kabbalist
Energy of the Hebrew Letters, The (Previously Power of the Aleph Beth Vols. 1 and 2)
Finding the Light Through the Darkness: Inspirational Lessons Rooted in the Bible and the Zohar
God Wears Lipstick: Kabbalah for Women
Holy Grail, The: A Manifesto on the Zohar
If You Don't Like Your Life, Change It!: Using Kabbalah to Rewrite the Movie of Your Life
Immortality: The Inevitability Of Eternal Life
Kabbalah Connection, The: Preparing the Soul For Pesach
Kabbalah for the Layman
Kabbalah Method, The: The Bridge Between Science and the Soul, Physics and Fulfillment, Quantum and the Creator
Kabbalah on the Sabbath: Elevating Our Soul to the Light
Kabbalah: The Power To Change Everything
Kabbalistic Astrology: And the Meaning of Our Lives
Kabbalistic Bible: Genesis
Kabbalistic Bible: Exodus
Kabbalistic Bible: Leviticus
Kabbalistic Bible: Numbers
Kabbalistic Bible: Deuteronomy
Life Rules: How Kabbalah Can Turn Your Life From a Problem into a Solution
Living Kabbalah

BOOKS AVAILABLE AT

WWW. KABBALAH.COM/STORE

AND KABBALAH CENTRES AROUND THE WORLD

www.ingramcontent.com/pod-product-compliance
Lightning Source LLC
Chambersburg PA
CBHW020537100426
42813CB00038B/3473/J